Philip Henry Wicksteed

Dante

Six sermons

Philip Henry Wicksteed

Dante
Six sermons

ISBN/EAN: 9783743350151

Manufactured in Europe, USA, Canada, Australia, Japa

Cover: Foto ©Lupo / pixelio.de

Manufactured and distributed by brebook publishing software
(www.brebook.com)

Philip Henry Wicksteed

Dante

DANTE

DANTE

SIX SERMONS

BY

PHILIP H. WICKSTEED, M.A.

Author of "The Alphabet of Economic Science," &c.

London

PUBLISHED BY ELKIN MATHEWS

IN VIGO STREET, W.

Dante : Six Sermons
Post 8vo., 158 pp., Price 6s.)
Kegan Paul, 1879 ·

Second Ed. (Crown 8vo., 122 pp., Price 2s.)
Elkin Mathews, 1890

Third Ed. (Crown 8vo., Price 2s. net)
Elkin Mathews & John Lane, 1892

Fourth Ed., (Crown 8vo., Price 2s. net)
Elkin Mathews, March, 1895
(Unaltered reprint)

Fifth Ed., (Crown 8vo., Price 2s. net)
Elkin Mathews
(Unaltered reprint)

CONTENTS.

PREFACE TO THE THIRD EDITION.

THE demand for the "Six Sermons" still continues; and
therefore reissue them essentially unchanged. A few
ifications and warnings have been introduced in the
notes, and a very few corrections of detail into the text.

While increasingly conscious of their defects, both in
form and substance, I still feel, after thirteen years of
continued study, that they present, essentially, what I
should wish to emphasise in a first book on Dante.

P. H. W.

May, 1892.

The five Sermons which form the body of this little book on Dante were delivered in the ordinary course of my ministry at Little Portland Street Chapel, in the autumn of 1878, and subsequently at the Free Christian Church, Croydon, in a slightly altered form.

They are now printed, at the request of many of my hearers, almost exactly as delivered at Croydon.

The substance of a sixth Sermon has been thrown into an Appendix.

* * * * * * * * *

The translations I have given are sometimes paraphrastic, and virtually contain glosses or interpretations which make it necessary to warn the reader against regarding them as in every case Dante's *ipsissima verba.* For the most part the renderings are substantially my own ; but I have freely availed myself of numerous translations, without special acknowledgment, whenever they supplied me with suitable phrases.

I have only to add the acknowledgment of my obligations to Fraticelli's edition of Dante's works (whose numbering of the minor poems and the letters I have adopted for reference), to the same writer's 'Life of Dante,' and to Mr. Symonds's ' Introduction to the Study of Dante.'

P. H. W.

June, 1879.

PREFACE TO THE SECOND EDITION.

The increasing frequency of demands for this volume, which has long been out of print, has induced me to reissue it.

Slight as it is, it has been found to have a certain value as a first book on Dante, which may give those who go no further some conception of what the Comedy means, and may help others to approach its study from the point of view of *life*, rather than that of literature and scholarship in the narrower sense.

In this edition a few corrections of detail have been introduced, and an index of passages added.

P. H. W.

June, 1890.

I.

DANTE'S LIFE AND PRINCIPLES

I. AS A CITIZEN OF FLORENCE

THERE are probably few competent judges who would hesitate to give Dante a place of honour in the triad of the world's greatest poets; and amongst these three Dante occupies a position wholly his own, peerless and unapproached in history.

For Homer and Shakespeare reflect the ages in which they lived, in all their fulness and variety of life and motive, largely sinking their own individuality in the intensity and breadth of their sympathies. They are great teachers doubtless, and fail not to lash what they regard as the growing vices or follies of the day, and to impress upon their hearers the solemn lessons of those inevitable facts of life which they epitomise and vivify. But their teaching is chiefly incidental or indirect, it is largely unconscious and is often almost as difficult to unravel from their works as it is from the life and nature they so faithfully reflect.

With Dante it is far otherwise. Aglow with a prophet's passionate conviction, an apostle's undying zeal, he is guided by a philosopher's breadth and clearness of principle, a poet's unfailing sense of beauty and command of emotions, to a social reformer's definite and pratical aims and a mystic's peace of religious communion. And, though his works abound in dramatic touches of startling power and variety,

3

and delineations of character unsurpassed in delicacy, yet with all the depth and scope of his sympathies he never for a moment losses himself or forgets his purpose.

As a philosopher and statesman, he had analysed with keen precision the social institutions, the political forces, and the historical antecedents by which he found his time and country dominated; as a moralist, a theologian, and a man, he had grasped with a firmness that nothing could relax the essential conditions of human blessedness here and hereafter, and with an intensity and fixity of definite self-conscious purpose almost without parallel, he threw the passionate energy of his nature into the task of preaching the eternal truth to his countrymen, and through them to the world, and thwarting and crushing the powers and institutions which he regarded as hostile to the well-being of mankind. He strove to teach his brothers that their true bliss lay in the exercise of virtue here, and the blessed vision of God hereafter. And as a step towards this, and an essential part of its realisation, he strove to make Italy one in heart and tongue, to raise her out of the sea of petty jealousies and intrigues in which she was plunged; in a word, to erect her into a free, united country, with a noble mother tongue. These two purposes were one; and, supported and supplemented by a never-dying zeal for truth, a never-failing sense of beauty, they inspired the life and works of Dante Alighieri.

It is often held and taught, that a strong and definite didactic purpose must inevitably be fatal to the highest forms of art, must clip the wings of poetic imagination, distort the symmetry of poetic sympathy, and substitute hard and angular contrasts for the melting grace of those curved lines of beauty which pass one into the other. Had Dante never lived, I know not where we should turn for the decisive refutation of this thought; but in Dante it is the very combination said to be impossible that inspires and enthrals us. A perfect artist, guided in the exercise of his art by an unflagging intensity of moral purpose; a prophet, submitting his inspirations to the keenest philosophical analysis, pouring them into the most finished artistic moulds, yet bringing them into ever fresher and fuller contact with their living source; a moralist and philosopher whose thoughts are fed by a prophet's directness of vision and a poet's tender grace of love, a poet's might and subtlety of imagination—Philosopher, Prophet, Poet, supreme as each, unique as a combination of them all—such was Dante Alighieri! And his voice will never be drowned or forgotten as long as man is dragged downward by passion, and struggles upward towards God, as long as he that sows to the flesh shall of the flesh reap corruption, and he that sows to the spirit reaps of the spirit life everlasting, as long as the heart of man can glow responsive to a holy indignation with wrong, or can feel the sweetness of the harmonics of peace.

It is little that I can hope to do, and yet I would fain do something, towards opening to one here and there some glimpse into that mighty temple, instinct with the very presence of the Eternal, raised by the master hand, nay rather wrought out of the mighty heart of Dante; but before we can even attempt to identify a few fragments of the "Divine Comedy," as landmarks to guide us, in our turn, through Hell and Purgatory up to Heaven, it is needful for us to have some conception who Dante Alighieri was, and what were his fortunes in this mortal life.

And here I must once for all utter a warning, and thereby discharge myself of a special duty. The Old Testament itself has not been more ruthlessly allegorised than have Dante's works and even his very life. The lack of trustworthy materials, in any great abundance, for an account of the poet's outward lot, the difficulty of fixing with certainty when he is himself relating actual events and when his apparent narratives are merely allegorical, the obscurity, incompleteness, and even apparent inconsistency of some of the data he supplies, the uncertainty as to the exact time at which his different works were composed and the precise relation in which they stand to each other, and the doubts which have been thrown upon the authenticity of some of the minor documents upon which the poet's biographers generally rely, have all combined to involve almost every step of his life in deep obscurity. Here, then, is a field upon which laborious research, ingenious conjecture, and wild speculation can find unending employment, and consequently every branch of the study has quite a literature of its own.

Now into this mass of controversial and speculative writings on Dante, I do not make the smallest pretensions to have penetrated a single step. I am far from wishing to disparage such studies, or to put forward in my own defence that stale and foolish plea, the refuge of pretentious ignorance in every region of inquiry, that a mind coming fresh to the study has the advantage over those that are already well versed in it; but surely the students who are making the elucidation of Dante their life work would not ask or wish, that until their endless task is completed all those whose souls have been touched by the direct utterance of the great poet, should hold their peace until qualified to speak by half a life of study.

With no further apology, then, for seeming to venture too rashly on the task, we may go on to a brief sketch of Dante's life and principles. The main lines which I shall follow are in most cases traced distinctly enough by Dante's own hand, and to the best of my belief, they represent a fair average of the present or recent conclusions of scholars; but, on the other hand, there have always been some who would unhesitatingly treat as allegory much of what I shall present to you as fact; who for instance would treat all Dante's love for Beatrice, and indeed Beatrice's very existence, as purely allegorical; and, again, where the allegory is admitted on all hands, there is a ceaseless shifting and endless variety in the special interpretations adopted and rejected by the experts.

Dante, or properly Durante Alighieri was born in Florence of an ancient and, perhaps, noble family, in the

year 1265. We may note that his life falls in a period
which we used to be taught to regard as an age of intellectual
stagnation and social barbarism, in which Christianity had
degenerated into a jumbled chaos of puerile and immoral
superstitions. We may note also that in the early years of
his life the poet was a contemporary of some of the noblest
representatives of the pseudo-Catholic civilisation, that is to
say of mediæval philosophy, theology, and chivalry, while
his manhood was joined in loving friendship with the first
supremely great mediæval artist, and before he died one
of the great precursors and heralds of the revival of learning
was growing up to manhood, and another had already left his
cradle. To speak of Roger Bacon, Thomas Aquinas, and St.
Louis, as living when Dante was born, of Giotto as his
companion and friend, of Petrarch and Boccaccio as already
living when he died, is to indicate more clearly than could
be done by any more elaborate statement, the position he
occupies at the very turning point of the Middle Ages, when
the forces of modern life had begun to rise, but the
supremacy of mediæval faith and discipline was as yet
unbroken. Accordingly Dante, in whom the truest spirit of
the age is, as it were, "made flesh," may be variously
regarded as the great morning star of modern enlightenment,
freedom, and culture, or as the very type of mediæval
discipline, faith, and chivalry. To me, I confess, this latter
aspect of Dante's life is altogether predominant. To me he
is the very incarnation of Catholicism, not in its shame, but
in its glory. Yet the future is always contained in the

present when rightly understood, and just because Dante was the perfect representative of his own age, he became the herald and the prophecy of the ages to come, not, as we often vainly imagine them, rebelling against and escaping from the overshadowing solemnity of the ages past, but growing out of them as their natural and necessary result.

In the year 1265, then, Dante, was born in Florence, then one of the most powerful and flourishing, but also, alas! one of the most factious and turbulent of the cities of Europe. He was not nine years old when he first met that Beatrice Portinari who became thenceforth the loadstar of his life. As to this lady we have little to say. The details which Dante's early biographers give us add but little to our knowledge of her, and so far as they are not drawn from the poet's own words, are merely such graceful commonplaces of laudatory description as any imagination of ordinary capacity would spontaneously supply for itself. When we have said that Beatrice was a beautiful, sweet, and virtuous girl, we have said all that we know, or all that we need care to know, of the daughter of Folco Portinari, who lived, was married, and died in Florence at the end of the thirteenth century. All that she is to us more than other Florentine maidens, she is to us through that poet who, as he wept her untimely death, hoped with no vain hope "to write of her, what ne'er was writ of woman." [1]

It puts no great strain on our powers of credence, to

[1] *Vita Nuova* xliii.

accept Dante's own statement of the rush of almost
stupifying emotions which overwhelmed his childish heart
when (to follow Boccaccio's account) he went with his father
to Portinari's house, and was sent to play with other children,
amongst them the little Beatrice, a child of eight years old.
The "New Life" waked within him from that moment and
its strength and purity made him strong and pure.[1]

Nine more years have passed. Dante is now eighteen.
He has made rapid progress in all the intellectual and
personal accomplishments which are held to adorn the
position of a Florentine gentleman. His teachers have in
some cases already discerned the greatness of his powers, and
he has become aware, probably by essays which never saw
the light, that he has not only a poet's passions and
aspirations, but a poet's power of moulding language into
oneness with his thought. He and Beatrice know each
other by sight, as neighbours or fellow-citizens, but Dante
has never heard her voice address a word to him. Yet she
is still the centre of all his thoughts. She has never ceased
to be to him the perfect ideal of growing womanhood, and
to his devout and fervid imagination, just because she is the
very flower of womanly courtesy, grace, and virtue, she is an
angel upon earth. Not in the hackneyed phrase of compli-
mentary commonplace, not in the exaggerated cant of
would-be poetical metaphor, but in the deep verity of his
inmost life, Dante Alighieri believes that Beatrice Portinari,

[1] *Vita Nuova* i, ii.

the maiden whose purity keeps him pure, whose grace and beauty are as guardian angels watching over his life, has more of heaven than of earth about her, and claims kindred with God's more perfect family.

Beatrice is now seventeen, she is walking with two companions in a public place, she meets Dante, and allows herself to utter a few words of graceful greeting. It is the first time she has spoken to him, and Dante's soul is thrilled and fired to its very depths. Not many hours afterwards, the poet began the first of his sonnets that we still possess, perhaps the first he ever wrote.[1]

Let us pass over eight or nine years more. Dante, now about twenty-six, is the very flower of chivalry and poetry. The foremost men in his own and other cities—artists, musicians, poets, scholars, and statesmen—are his friends. Somewhat hard of access and reserved, but the most fascinating of companions and the faithfulest of friends to those who have found a real place in his heart, Dante takes a rank of acknowledged eminence amongst the poets of his day. His verses, chiefly in praise of Beatrice, are written in a strain of tender sentiment, that gives little sign of what is ultimately to come out of him, but there is a nervous and concentrated power of diction, a purity and elevation of conception in them, which may not have been obvious to his companions as separating him from them, but which to eyes instructed by the result is full of deepest meaning.

[1] *Vita Nuova*, iii. ; *Inferno*, xv. 55, sqq. &c.

And what of Beatrice? She is dead. It was never given to Dante to call her his. We know not so much as whether he even aspired to more than that gracious salutation in which, to use his own expression, he seemed to touch "the very limits of beatitude." [1]

Be this as it may, it is certain that Beatrice (if we may accept Boccaccio's authority and identify her with Beatrice Portinari) married a powerful citizen of Florence several years before her death. But she was still the guardian angel of the poet's life, she was still the very type of womanhood to him ; and there was not a word or thought of his towards her but was full of utter courtesy and purity. And now, in the flower of her loveliness she is cut down by death, and to Dante life has become a wilderness. [2]

Yet eight or nine years more. Dante is now in what his philosophical system regards as the very prime of life. [3] He is thirty-five. The date is 1300. Since we left him weeping for the death of Beatrice, the unity of his life has been shattered and he has lost his way, but only for a time. Now his powers and purposes are richer, stronger, more concentrated than ever.

In his first passion of grief for Beatrice's death he had been profoundly touched by the pity of a gentle-eyed damsel whom a far from groundless conjecture identifies with Gemma Donati, the lady whom he married not long afterwards. With this Gemma he lived till his banishment, and

[1] *Vita Nuova*, iii.   [2] *Vita Nuova*, iv.-xxx.   [3] *Convito*, iv. 23.

they had a numerous family. The internal evidence of Dante's works, and the few circumstances really known to us, give little support to the tradition that their marriage was an unhappy one.

Dante's friends, says Boccaccio, had hoped that domestic peace might console him for his irreparable loss, but he himself had rather sought for consolation in the study of philosophy and theology ; and it befel him, he tells us, as one who in seeking silver strikes on gold—not, haply, without guidance from on high ;—for he began to see many things as in a dream, and dreamed that Dame Philosophy must needs be supreme ! [1]

But neither domestic nor literary cares and duties absorbed his energies. In late years he had begun to take an active part in the politics of his city, and was now fast rising to his true position as one of the foremost men of Florence and of Italy.

Thus we see new interests and new powers rising in his life, but for a time the unity of that life was gone. While Beatrice lived, Dante's whole being was centred in her, and she was to him the visible token of God's presence upon earth, the living proof of the reality and the beauty of things Divine, born to fill the world with faith and gentleness. But when she was gone, when other passions and pursuits disputed with her memory the foremost place in Dante's heart, it was as though he had lost the secret and the meaning of life, as though he had lost the guidance of Heaven,

[1] *Convito*, ii. 13.

and was whirled helplessly in the vortex of moral, social, and
political disorder which swept over his country. For Italian
politics at this period form a veritable chaos of shifting
combinations and entanglements, of plots and counterplots,
of intrigue and treachery and vacillation, though lightened
ever and again by gleams of noblest patriotism and devotion.

Yet Dante's soul was far too strong to be permanently
overwhelmed. Gradually his philosophical reflections began
to take definite shape. He felt the wants of his own life and
of his country's life. He pierced down to the fundamental
conditions of political and social welfare; and when human
philosophy had begun to restore unity and concentration to
his powers, then the sweet image of the pure maiden who
had first waked his soul to love returned glorified and transfigured to guide him into the very presence of God. She
was the symbol of Divine philosophy. She, and she only
could restore his shattered life to unity and strength, and the
love she never gave him as a woman, she could give him as
the protecting guardian of his life, as the vehicle of God's
highest revelation.[1]

With his life thus strengthened, and enriched, with a firm
heart and a steady purpose, Dante Alighieri stood in the year
1300 at the helm of the State of Florence. And here accordingly it becomes necessary for us to dwell for a moment on
some of the chief political forces with which he had to deal.

The two great factions of the Guelfs and Ghibellines were
tearing the very heart of Italy; and without going into any

[1] *Vita Nuova*, xxi.-xliii. ; *Convito*, ii. ; *Purgatorio*, xxx., xxxi.

detail, we must try to point out the central ideas of each party. The Ghibellines, then, appear to have represented an aristocratic principle of order, constantly in danger of becoming oppressive, while the Guelfs represented a democratic principle of progress, ever verging upon chaotic and unbridled licence. The Ghibellines longed for a national unity, resting on centralisation; the Guelfs aimed at a local independence which tended to national disintegration. The Ghibellines, regarding the German Empire as the heir and representative of the Empire of Rome, and as the symbol of Italian unity, espoused the Emperor's cause against the Pope, declared the temporal power independent of the spiritual, and limited the sphere of the priests entirely to the latter. The Guelfs found in the political action of the Pope a counterpoise to the influence of the Emperor; the petty and intriguing spirit of the politics of the Vatican made its ruler the natural ally of the disintegrating Guelfs rather than the centralising Ghibellines, and accordingly the Guelfs ardently espoused the cause of the Pope's temporal power, and often sought in the royal house of France a further support against Germany.

These broad lines, however, were constantly blurred and crossed by personal intrigue or ambition, by family jealousies, feuds, and rivalries, by unnatural alliances or by corruption and treachery.

Now Dante was by family tradition a Guelf. Florence too was nominally the headquarters of Guelfism, and Dante had fought bravely in her battles against the Ghibellines.

But the more he reflected upon the sources of the evils by which Italy was torn, the more profoundly he came to distrust the unprincipled meddling of the greedy princes of the house of France in Italian politics, and the more jealously did he watch the temporal power of the Pope. Perhaps the political opinions he afterwards held were not as yet fully consolidated, but his votes and proposals—which we read with a strange interest in the city archives of Florence nearly six hundred years after the ink has dried—show that in 1300 he was at any rate on the highway to the conclusions he ultimately reached. And we may therefore take this occasion of stating what they were.

It appeared to Dante that Italy was sunk in moral, social, and political chaos, for want of a firm hand to repress the turbulent factions that rent her bosom; and that no hand except an Emperor's could be firm enough. The empire of Rome was to him the most imposing and glorious spectacle offered by human history. God had guided Rome by miracles and signs to the dominion of the world that the world might be at peace.

And parallel with this temporal Empire founded by Julius Cæsar, was the spiritual Empire of the Church, founded by Jesus Christ. Both alike were established by God for the guidance of mankind : to rebel against either was to rebel against God. Brutus and Cassius, who slew Julius Cæsar, the embodiment of the Empire, are placed by Dante in the same depth of Hell as Judas Iscariot, who betrayed Jesus Christ, the founder of the Church.[1] These three had done

---

[1] *Inferno*, xxxiv. 55-67.

what in them lay to reduce the world to civil and religious chaos, for they had compassed the death of the ideal representatives of civil and religious order. But both powers alike laid a mighty trust upon the human agents who administered them; and as the Empire and the Church were the sublimest and the holiest of ideal institutions, so a tyrannical Emperor and a corrupt or recreant Pope were amongst the foulest of sinners, to be rebuked and resisted with every power of body and soul.

Dante could no more conceive of the spiritual life without the authoritative guidance of the all-present, all-pervading Church, than he could conceive of a well-ordered polity without the all-penetrating force of law. But it appeared to him as monstrous for the Pope to seek political influence and to use his spiritual powers for political ends as he would have judged it for the Emperor to exercise spiritual tyranny over the faith of Christians.[1]

There can have been little in the political life of Florence at this time to attract one who held such views. But Dante of all men hated and despised weak shrinking from responsibility. If there is one feature in his stern character more awful than any other, it is his unutterable, withering contempt for those who lived without praise or blame, those wretches who never were alive. He saw them afterwards in the outer circle of Hell, mingled with that caitiff herd of angels who were not for God, and yet were not for the rebels, but were only for themselves.

[1] See the *De Monarchia.* Compare *Purgatorio,* xvi. 103-112 ; *Paradiso,* xviii. 124-136.

Heaven drove them forth, Heaven's beauty not to stain,
Nor would the deep Hell deign to have them there
For any glory that the damned might gain !

No fame of them survives upon the earth, Pity and
Justice hold them in disdain, their cries of passion and of
woe are ever whirled through the starless air, and their forgotten lot appears to them so base that they envy the very
torments of the damned. "Let us not speak of them,"
says Virgil to Dante, "but gaze and pass them by." [1]

So Dante shrank not from his task when called to public
office, but laid his strong hand upon the helm of Florence.
During a part of this year 1300, he filled the supreme
magistracy, and at that very time the old disputes of Guelf
and Ghibelline broke out in the city afresh under a thin
disguise. We have seen that Dante's sympathies were now
almost completely Ghibelline, but as the first Prior of Florence
his duty was firmly to suppress all factious attempts to disturb
the city's peace and introduce intestine discord. It was not
by party broils that Italy would be restored to peace and
harmony. He behaved with a more than Roman fortitude,
for it is easier for a father to chastise a rebellious son than
for a true friend to override the claims of friendship. Dante's
dearest friend, Guido Cavalcanti, bound to him by every tie
of sympathy and fellowship which could unite two men in
common purposes and common hopes, was one of the leaders
of the party with which Dante himself sympathised; and
yet, for the good of his country and in obedience to his

[1] *Inferno*, iii. 22-51.

magisterial duty, he tore this friend from his side though not from his heart, and pronounced on him the sentence of banishment, the weight of which he must even then have known so well. It speaks to the eternal honour of Guido, as well as Dante, that this deed appears not to have thrown so much as a shadow upon the friendship of the two men.[1]

Had Dante's successors in office dealt with firmness and integrity equal to his own, all might have been well; but a vacillating and equivocal policy soon opened the door to suspicions and recriminations; Florence ceased to steer her own course and permitted foreign interference with her affairs; while the Pope, with intentions that might have been good, but with a policy which proved utterly disastrous, furthered the intervention of the French Prince, Charles of Valois. It was a critical moment. An embassy to the Papal Court was essential, and a firm hand must meanwhile hold the reins at Florence. "If I go, who shall stay? if I stay, who shall go?" Dante is reported to have said, and though the saying is probably apocryphal, yet it points out happily enough the true position of affairs. Dante was now no longer the chief magistrate of his city, but he was in fact, though not in name, the one man of Florence, the one man of Italy.[2]

Finally he resolved to go to Rome. But the blindness or corruption of the Papal Court was invincible; and while

[1] Compare *Inferno*, x. 52-72, 109-111.

[2] It is questioned by many recent scholars whether the part played by Dante in the political history of his times was as important as has usually been supposed, and as is here represented.—1890.

Dante was still toiling at his hopeless task, Charles of Valois entered Florence, couching the lance wherewith Judas tilted,[1] soon to realise the worst suspicions of those who had opposed his intervention. Nominally a restorer of tranquillity, he stirred up all the worst and most lawless passions of the Florentines; and while Dante was serving his country at Rome, the unjust and cruel sentence of banishment was launched against him, his property was confiscated and seized; a few months afterwards he was sentenced to be burned to death should he ever fall into the power of the Florentines, and, not content with all this, his enemies heaped upon his name the foulest calumnies of embezzlement and malversation—calumnies which I suppose no creature from that hour to this has ever for one moment believed, but which could not fail to make the envenomed wound strike deeper into Dante's heart.

So now he must leave "all things most dear—this the first arrow shot from exile's bow," in poverty and dependence his proud spirit must learn "how salt a taste cleaves to a patron's bread, how hard a path mounts and descends a patron's stair;" and, above all, his unsullied purity and patriotism must find itself forced into constant association or even alliance with selfish and personal ambition, or with tyranny, meanness, and duplicity.[2] How that great soul bore itself amid all these miseries, what it learnt from them, where it sought and found a refuge from them, we shall see when we take up again the broken thread which we must drop to-day.

[1] *Purgatorio*, xx. 73-74.   [2] *Paradiso*, xvii. 55-63.

II

DANTE'S LIFE AND PRINCIPLES

II. IN EXILE

A RAPID sketch of the most decisive events and the leading motives of the life of Dante Alighieri has brought us to the eventful period of his Priorate in 1300 and his banishment in 1302. His unsuccessful efforts to carry out a firm and statesmanlike policy in Florence, with the wreck of his own fortunes consequent upon their failure, may be regarded as the occasion if not the cause of his conceiving his greatest work, the "Divine Comedy."

Nineteen years elapsed between Dante's exile and his death. They were years of varied hope, aspiration and endeavour, but, as they advanced, the main strength of the poet's life was concentrated more and more upon the work already conceived in the years of mourning for Beatrice. "Forging on the anvil of incessant toil" the several parts of his great work, and "welding them into imperishable symmetry,"[1] the might of his intellect and the passion of his heart grappled for nineteen years with the task of giving worthy utterance to his vast idea. Line by line, canto by canto, the victory was won. Dante had shown that his mother tongue could rise to loftier themes than Greek or Roman had ever touched, and had wrought out the fitting garb of a poem that stands alone in the literature of the world in the scope and sublimity of its conception.

[1] Symonds.

Barely to realise what it was that Dante attempted, wakes feelings in our hearts akin to awe. When we think of that work and of the man who, knowing what it was, deliberately set himself to do it, an appalling sense of the presence of overwhelming grandeur falls upon us, as when a great wall of rocky precipice rises sheer at our side, a thousand and yet a thousand feet towards heaven. Our heads swim as we gaze up to the sky-line of such a precipice, the ground seems to drop from beneath our feet, all our past and present becomes a dream, and our very hold of life seems to slip away from us. But the next moment a great exultation comes rushing upon our hearts; with quickened pulses and drawing deeper breath we rise to the sublimity of the scene around us, and our whole being is expanded and exalted by it. After holding converse with such grandeur our lives can never be so small again. And so it is when the meaning of Dante's Comedy breaks upon us. When we follow the poet step by step as he beats or pours his thoughts into language, when we note the firmness of his pace, the mastery with which he handles and commands his infinite theme, the unflinching directness, the god-like self-reliance, with which he lays bare the hearts of his fellow-men and makes himself the mouth-piece of the Eternal, when we gaze upon his finished work and the despair of Hell, the yearning of Purgatory, the peace of Heaven, sweep over our hearts, we are ready to whisper in awe-struck exultation :

> What immortal hand or eye
> Dared form thy fearful symmetry?

The allegory with which the "Divine Comedy" opens, shadows forth the meaning and the purpose of the whole poem. In interpreting it we may at first give prominence to its political signification, not because its main intention is certainly or probably political, but because we shall thus be enabled to pass in due order from the outer to the inner circle of the poet's beliefs and purposes.[1]

In the year 1300, then, Dante Alighieri found that he had wandered, he knew not how, from the true path of life, and was plunged into the deadly forest of political, social, and moral disorder which darkened with terrific shade the fair soil of Italy. Deep horror settled upon the recesses of his heart during the awful night, but at last he saw the fair light of the morning sun brightening the shoulders of a hill that stretched above : this was the peaceful land of moral and political order, which seemed to offer an escape from the bitterness of that ghastly forest. Gathering heart at this sweet sight, Dante set himself manfully to work, with the nether foot ever planted firmly on the soil, to scale that glorious height. But full soon his toilsome path would be disputed with him. The dire powers of Guelfism would not allow the restoration of peace and order to Italy. His first foe was the incurable factiousness and lightness of his own fair Florence. Like a lithe and speckled panther it glided before him to oppose his upward progress, and forced

---

[1] I should not now venture to give even this secondary promin-ence to the political, as distinct from the moral, significance of the "three beasts."—1892.

him once and again to turn back upon his steps towards that dread forest he had left. But though forced back, Dante could not lose hope. Might he not tame this wild but beauteous beast? Yes; he might have coped with the fickle, lustful, factious, envious but lovely Florence, had not haughty France rushed on him like a lion, at whose voice the air must tremble, had not lean and hungry Rome, laden with insatiable greed, skulked wolf-like in his path. It was the wolf above all that forced him back into the sunless depths of that forest of dismay, and dashed to the ground his hopes of gaining the fair height. When could he, when could his Italy, rise from this chaos and be at peace? Not till some great political Messiah should draw his sword. With no base love of pelf or thirst for land, but fed with wisdom, love and virtue, he should exalt low-lying Italy and drive away her foes. Like a noble hound, he should chase the insatiable wolf of Roman greed from city to city back to the Hell from which it came.[1]

Dante's hope in this political Messiah rose and fell, but never died in his heart. Now with the gospel of Messianic peace, now with the denunciation of Messianic judgment on his lips, he poured out his lofty enthusiasm in those apostolic and prophetic letters, some few of which survive amidst the wrecks of time as records of his changing moods and his unchanging purposes.

Now one and now another of the Ghibelline leaders may have seemed to Dante from time to time to be the hero, the

[1] See *Inferno*, i. 1-111.

Messiah, for whom he waited. But again and yet again his hopes were crushed and blighted, and the panther, the lion and the wolf, still cut off the approach to that fair land.

More than once the poet's hopes may have hung upon the fortunes of the mighty warrior Uguccione, whose prodigies of valour rivalled the fabled deeds of the knights of story. To this man Dante was bound by ties of closest friendship. To him he is said to have dedicated the Inferno, the first cantica of his Comedy, and it has even been maintained that he was that hero "'twixt the two Feltros born"[1] to whom Dante once looked to slay the wolf of Rome.

Far higher probably, and certainly far better grounded, were the poet's earlier hopes when Henry VII. of Germany descended into Italy to bring order into her troubled states. To Dante, as we have seen, the Emperor was Emperor of Rome and not of Germany. He was Cæsar's successor, the natural representative of Italian unity, the Divinely-appointed guardian of civil order. With what passionate yearning Dante looked across the Alps for a deliverer, how large a part of the woes of Italy he laid at the feet of Imperial neglect, may be gathered from many passages in his several works; but nowhere do these thoughts find stronger utterance than in the sixth canto of the Purgatory. The poet sees the shades of Virgil and the troubadour Sordello join in a loving embrace at the bare mention of the name of Mantua, where both of them were born. "O Italy!" he cries, "thou slave! thou hostelry of woe! ship without

1 *Inferno*, i. 105.—More correctly referred to Can Grande of Verona.

helmsman, in the tempest rude! No queen of provinces, but house of shame! See how that gentle soul, e'en at the sweet sound of his country's name, was prompt to greet his fellow-citizen. Then see thy living sons, how one with other ever is at war, and whom the self-same wall and moat begird, gnaw at each other's lives. Search, wretched one, along thy sea-bound coasts, then inward turn to thine own breast, and see if any part of thee rejoice in peace. Of what avail Justinian's curb of law, with none to stride the saddle of command, except to shame thee more? Alas! ye priests, who should be at your prayers, leaving to Cæsar the high seat of rule, did ye read well the word of God to you, see ye not how the steed grows wild and fell by long exemption from the chastening spur, since that ye placed your hands upon the rein? O German Albert! who abandonest, wild and untamed, the steed thou should'st bestride, may the just sentence from the stars above fall on thy race in dire and open guise, that he who follows thee may see and fear. For, drawn by lust of conquest otherwhere, thou and thy sire, the garden of the empire have ye left a prey to desolation. Come, thou insensate one, and see the Montagues and Capulets, Monaldi, Philippeschi, for all whom the past has sadness or the future fear. Come, come, thou cruel one, and see oppression trampling on thy faithful ones, and heal their ills. . . . . Come thou and see thy Rome, who weeps for thee, a lonely widow crying day and night, 'My Cæsar, wherefore hast thou left me thus?' Come, see how love here governs every heart! Or, if our sorrows move thee

not at all, blush for thine own fair fame.—Nay, let me say
it : O Thou God Most High, Thou Who wast crucified for us
on earth, are Thy just eyes turned otherwhither now ? Or
in the depths of counsel dost Thou work for some good end,
clean cut off from our ken ? For all Italia's lands are
full of tyrants, and every hind—so he be factious—grows
Marcellus-high."[1]

Such was the cry for deliverance which went up from
Dante's heart to the Emperor. Picture his hopes when
Henry VII. came with the blessing of the Pope, who had had
more than his fill of French influence at last, to bring peace
and order into Italy ; picture the exultation with which he
learnt alike from Henry's deeds and words that he was just,
impartial, generous, and came not as a tyrant, not as a party
leader, but as a firm and upright ruler to restore prosperity
and peace ; picture his indignation when the incurable
factiousness and jealousies of the Italian cities, and of
Florence most of all, thwarted the Emperor at every step ;
picture the bitterness of his grief when, after struggling nigh
three years in vain, Henry fell sick and died at Buonconvento.
In Paradise the poet saw the place assigned "to Henry's
lofty soul—his who should come to make the crooked straight.
ere Italy was ready for his hand ;" but the dream of his
throne on earth was broken for ever.[2]

Henry died in 1313. This blow was followed by the
fall of Uguccione when he seemed almost on the point of

---

[1] *Purgatorio*, vi. 76-126.
[2] See especially *Epistolae*, v-vii. ; *Paradiso*, xxx. 133-138.

realising some of Dante's dearest hopes. The poet and the warrior alike found refuge at Verona now, with Can Grande della Scala, to whom Dante dedicated the third cantica of his Comedy, the Paradise.[1] Did the exile's hopes revive again at the Court of Verona? Did the gallant and generous young soldier whose gracious and delicate hospitality called out such warm affection from his heart,[2] seem worthy to accomplish that great mission in which Uguccione and Henry had failed? It is more than probable that such thoughts found room in Dante's sorrow-laden heart. And yet we cannot but suppose that while his certainty remained unshaken that in God's good time the deliverer would come, yet the hopes which centred in any single man must have had less and less assurance in them as disappointment after disappointment came.

Be this as it may, near the close of his life Dante was still able to make Beatrice testify of him in the courts of Heaven : "Church militant has not a son stronger in hope than he. God knows it."[3] Simple as these words are, yet by him who has scanned Dante's features and pondered on his life, they may well be numbered amongst those moving and strengthening human utterances that ring like a trumpet through the ages and call the soul to arms.

But were Dante's hopes all concentrated on the advent

---

[1] See Epistola xi. [2] *Paradiso*, xvii. 70-93. [3] *Ibid.* xxv. 52-54. In this passage, however, "Hope," as appears from the context, is used only in this special sense of the "sure and certain hope" of eternal bliss.—1892.

of that political Messiah who was not to come in truth till our own day? Had it been so, the "Divine Comedy" would never have been born.

When Dante realised his own helplessness in the struggle against the panther of Florence, the lion of France, and the wolf of Rome, when he saw that to reorganise his country and remodel the social and political conditions of life would need the strong hand and the keen sword of some great hero raised by God, he also saw that for himself another way was opened, an escape from that wild forest into which his feet had strayed, an escape which it must be his task to point out to others, without which the very work of the hero for whom he looked would be in vain.

The deadly forest represented moral as well as political confusion; the sunlit mountain, moral as well as political order; and the beasts that cut off the ascent, moral as well as political foes to human progress.

From this moral chaos there was deliverance for every faithful soul, despite the lion and the wolf; and though the noble hound came not to chase the foul beasts back to Hell, yet was Dante led from the forest gloom even to the light of Heaven.

And how was he delivered? By Divine grace he saw Hell and Purgatory and Heaven—so was he delivered. He saw the souls of men stripped of every disguise, he saw their secret deeds of good or ill laid bare. He saw Popes and Emperors, ancient heroes and modern sages, the rich, the valiant, the noble, the fair of face, the sweet of voice; and no longer dazzled, no longer overawed, he saw them as they were, he saw their deeds, he saw the fruits of them. So was he delivered from the entanglements and perplexities, from the delusions and seductions of the world, so were his feet set upon the rock, so did he learn to sift the true from the false, to rise above all things base and set his soul at peace, even when sorrow was gnawing his heart to death. He, while yet clothed in flesh and blood, went amongst the souls of the departed, "heard the despairing shrieks of spirits long immersed in woe, who wept each one the second death ; saw suffering souls contented in the flames, for each one looked to reach the realms of bliss, though long should be the time," and lastly he saw the souls in Heaven, and gazed upon the very light of God.[1]

All this he saw and heard under the guidance of human and Divine philosophy, symbolised, or rather concentrated and personified, in Virgil and Beatrice.

Of Virgil, and the unique position assigned to him in the Middle Ages, it is impossible here to speak at length. Almost from the first publication of the Æneid, and down to the time when the revival of learning reopened the treasures of Greek literature to Western Europe, Virgil reigned in the Latin countries supreme and unchallenged over the domain of poetry and scholarship. Within two generations of his own lifetime, altars were raised to him, by enthusiastic disciples, as to a diety. When Christianity spread, his supposed prediction of Christ in one of the

[1] *Inferno*, i. 112-129.

Eclogues endowed him with the character of a prophet ; and a magic efficacy had already been attributed to verses taken from his works. Throughout the Middle Ages, his fame still grew as the supreme arbiter in every field of literature, and as the repository of more than human knowledge, while fantastic legends clustered round his name as the great magician and necromancer. To Dante there must also have been a special fascination in the Imperial scope and sympathies of the Æneid ; for Virgil is pre-eminently the poet of the Roman Empire. But we must not pause to follow out this subject here. Suffice it that Dante felt for Virgil a reverence so deep, an admiration so boundless, and an affection so glowing, that he became to him the very type of human wisdom and excellence, the first agent of his rescue from the maze of passion and error in which his life had been entangled.

But Beatrice, the loved and lost, was the symbol and the channel of a higher wisdom, a diviner grace. She it was round whose sweet memory gathered the noblest purposes and truest wisdom of the poet's life. If ever he suffered the intensity of his devotion to truth and virtue for a moment to relax ; if ever, as he passed amongst luxurious courts, some siren voice soothed his cares with a moment of unworthy forgetfulness and ignoble ease ; if ever he suffered meaner cares or projects to draw him aside so much as in thought from his great mission, then it was Beatrice's glorified image that recalled him in tears of bitter shame and penitence to the path of pain, of effort, and of glory. It was her love that had rescued him from the fatal path ; Virgil was but her agent and emissary, and his mission was complete when he had led him to her. Human wisdom and virtue could guide him through Hell and Purgatory, could show him the misery of sin, and the need of purifying pain and fire, but it was only in Beatrice's presence that he could *feel* not only the utter hatefulness and shame of an unworthy life, but also the blessedness of heaven. [1]

Under the guidance of Virgil and Beatrice, then, Dante had seen Hell and Purgatory and Heaven. This had snatched his soul from death, had taught him, even in the midst of the moral and political chaos of his age, how to live and after what to strive. ' Could he show others what he himself had seen ? Could he save them, as he was saved, from the meanness, from the blindness, from the delusions of the life they led ? He could. Though it should be the toil of long and painful years, yet in the passionate conviction of his own experience he felt the power in him of making real to others what was so intensely real to him. But what did this involve ? The truth, if wholesome, was yet hard. He had dear and honoured friends whose lives had been stained by unrepented sin, and whose souls he had seen in Hell. Was he to cry aloud to all the world that these loved ones were amongst the damned, instead of tenderly hiding

[1] *Inferno*, i. 121-123, ii. 52-142 ; *Purgatorio*, xxx. sqq. ; *Paradiso*, passim.

their infirmities? Again, he was poor and an exile, he had lost "all things most dear," and was dependent for his very bread on the grace and favour of the great; yet if he told the world what he had seen, a storm of resentful hatred would crash upon him from every region of Italy. How would proud dames and lords brook to be told of their dead associates in sin and shame cursing their names from the very depths of Hell, and looking for their speedy advent there? How would pope and cardinal and monarch brook to be told by the powerless exile what he had heard from souls in Heaven, in Purgatory, and in Hell? E'en let them brook it as they might. His cry should be like the tempest that sweeps down upon the loftiest forest trees, but leaves the brushwood undisturbed. The mightiest in the land should hear his voice, and henceforth none should think that loftiness of place or birth could shield the criminal. He would tell in utter truth what he had seen. He knew what power was in him to brand the infamous with infamy that none could wash away, to rescue the fair memory of those the world had wrongfully condemned, to say what none but he dare say, in verse which none but he could forge, and bring all those who hearkened through Hell and Purgatory into Heaven.[1]

To deliver this message was the work of his life, the end to which all his studies were directed, from the time when it first became clear to his own mind till hard upon the day of

[1] *Paradiso*, xvii. 103-142.

his death. Hence his studious labours came to have a representative and vicarious character in his mind. He was proudly conscious that he lived and worked for mankind, and that his toil deserved the grateful recognition of his city and his country.

This trait in his character comes out with striking force in the noble letter which he wrote in answer to the proffered permission to return to his beloved Florence, but upon disgraceful conditions which he could not accept. The offer came when his fortunes were at their lowest ebb. Henry VII. was dead, Uguccione had lost his power. All hope of the exiles returning in triumph seemed at an end. Then came the offer of a pardon and recall, for which he had longed with all the passionate intensity of his nature. And yet it was but a mockery. It was a custom in Florence upon the Day of St. John the Baptist, the patron saint of the city, to release certain malefactors from the public gaols on their performing set acts of contrition; and a decree was passed that all the political exiles might return to their homes on St. John's Day in 1317, if they would pay a sum of money, walk in procession with tapers in their hands and with other tokens of guilt and penitence, to the church, and there offer themselves as ransomed malefactors to the saint.

Many of the exiles accepted the terms, but Dante's proud and indignant refusal shows us a spirit unbroken by disappointment and disaster, scorning to purchase ease by degradation. "Is this," he cries to the friend who communicated to him the conditions upon which he might return, "is this the glorious recall by which Dante Alighieri is summoned back to his country after well-nigh fifteen years of exile? Is this what innocence well-known to all, is this what the heavy toil of unbroken study, has deserved? Far be it from him who walks as her familiar with Philosophy to stoop to the base grovelling of a soul of clay and suffer himself thus to be treated like a vile malefactor. Far be it from the preacher of justice, when suffering outrage, to pay the acknowledgment of fair desert to the outrageous.

"Not by this path can I return. But let a way be found that hurts not Dante's honour and fair fame, and I will tread it with no tardy feet. If no such road leads back to Florence, then will I never enter Florence more. What! can I not gaze, wherever I may be, upon the mirror of sun and stars? Can I not ponder on the sweetest truths in any region under heaven, but I must first make myself base and vile before the people and the State of Florence?"[1]

Such was the answer of Dante Alighieri to that cruel insult which makes our cheeks glow even now with indignation. Such was the temper of the man who had seen Hell and Purgatory and Heaven, and who shrank not from the utterance of all that he had seen.

Dante must already have been engaged in writing the Comedy. Amongst the sufferings and burdens which were fast drawing him to the grave, amongst the agonies of indignation, of regret, of hope, of disappointment which still

[1] Epistola x.

racked his soul, the promise of the deep peace of God had already come upon him ; beneath a storm of passion at which our hearts quail was a calm of trustful self-surrender which no earthly power could disturb ; and ere long the harmonies of Paradise swelled in the poet's heart and sought for utterance in his last years.

But though his spirit was thus rapt to Heaven, he never lost his hold upon the earth ; never disdained to toil as best he might for the immediate instruction or well-being of his kind. More than once his eloquence and skill enabled him to render signal service to his protectors in conducting delicate negotiations, and at the same time to further that cause of Italian unity which was ever near his heart. Nor did the progress of his great work, the Comedy, altogether put an end to the varied subsidiary activity as a poet, a moralist, and a student of language and science, which had filled the earlier years of his exile.

One characteristic example of this by-work must suffice. In the last year but one of his life when he must have been meditating the last, perhaps the sublimest, cantos of the Paradise, when he might well have been excused if he had ceased to concern himself with any of the lower grades of truth, he heard a certain question of physics discussed and re-discussed, and never decided because of the specious but sophistical arguments which were allowed to veil it in doubt. The question was whether some portions of the sea are or are not on a higher level than some portions of the land ; and Dante, "nursed from his boyhood in the love of truth," as he

says, " could not endure to leave the question unresolved,
and determined to demonstrate the facts and to refute the
arguments alleged against them." [1] Accordingly he defended
his thesis on a Sunday in one of the churches of Verona
under the presidency of Can Grande.

This essay is a model of close reasoning and sound
scientific method, and the average nineteenth century reader,
with the average contempt for fourteenth century science,
would find much to reflect upon should he read and understand it. The vague and inconclusive style of reasoning
against which Dante contends is still rampant everywhere,
though its forms have changed ; while the firm grasp of
scientific method and the incisive reasoning of Dante himself
are still the exception in spite of all our modern training
in research.

Thus Dante was engaged to the last upon the whole field
of human thought. Such was the scope and power of his
mind that he could embrace at the same moment the very
opposite poles of speculation ; and such was his passion for
truth that, when gazing upon the very presence of God, he
could not bear to leave men in error when he could set them
right, though it were but as to the level of the land and sea.

But we must hasten to a close. Let us turn from the
consideration of Dante's work to a picture of personal
character drawn by his own hand. It is his ideal of a life

---

[1] *Quæstio de Aqua et Terra*, § 1. The authenticity of this treatise
is hotly disputed by many recent scholars.—1892.

inspired by that " gentleness " for which, since the days of
chivalry, we have had no precise equivalent in language,
and which is itself too rare in every age.

> The soul that this celestial grace adorns
> In secret holds it not ;
> For from the first, when she the body weds,
> She shows it, until death :
> Gentle, obedient, and alive to shame,
> Is seen in her first age,
> Adding a comely beauty to the frame,
> With all accomplishments :
> In youth is temperate and resolute,
> Replete with love and praise of courtesy,
> Placing in loyalty her sole delight :
> And in declining age
> Is prudent, just, and for her bounty known ;
> And joys within herself
> To listen and discourse of others' good :
> Then in the fourth remaining part of life
> To God is re-espoused,
> Contemplating the end that draws a-nigh,
> And blesseth all the reasons that are past ;
> —Reflect now, how the many are deceived ! ![1]

Cherishing such an ideal, Dante wandered from court
to court of Italy, finding here and there a heart of gold, but
for the most part moving amongst those to whom grace and
purity and justice were but names. Can we wonder that
sometimes the lonely exile felt as if his own sorrow-laden
heart were the sole refuge upon earth of love and temperance?

[1] Canzone xvi., ' Le dolci rime,' st. vii. See *Convito*, trat iv.
Translation slightly altered from Lyell.

Three noble dames, he tells us—noble in themselves but in nought else, for their garments were tattered, their feet unshod, their hair dishevelled, and their faces stained with tears—came and flung themselves at the portal of his heart, for they knew that Love was there. Moved with deep pity, Love came forth to ask them of their state. They were Rectitude, Temperance, and Generosity, once honoured by the world, now driven out in want and shame, and they came there for refuge in their woe. Then Love, with moistened eyes, bade them lift up their heads. If they were driven begging through the world, it was for men to weep and wail whose lives had fallen in such evil times; but not for them, hewn from the eternal rock—it was not for them to grieve. A race of men would surely rise at last whose hearts would turn to them again. And hearing thus how exiles great as these were grieved and comforted, the lonely poet thought his banishment his glory.

Yet when he looked for his sweet home and found it not, the agony that could not break his spirit fast destroyed his flesh, and he knew that death had laid the key upon his bosom.[1]

When this sublime and touching poem was composed we have no means of knowing, but it can hardly have been long before the end. When that end came, Dante can barely have completed his great life work, he can barely have written the last line of the " Divine Comedy." He had been on an unsuccessful mission in the service of his last protector,

[1] Canzone xix., 'Tre donne.'

D

Guido da Polenta of Ravenna. On his return he was seized
with a fatal illness, and died at Ravenna in 1321, at the age
of fifty-six.

Who can grudge him his rest ? As we read the four tracts
of the "Convito," which were to have been the first of fifteen,
but must now remain alone, as we are brought to a sudden
stand at the abrupt termination of his unfinished work on
the dialects and poetry of Italy,[1] as we ponder on the
unexhausted treasures that still lay in the soul of him who
could write as Dante wrote even to the end, we can hardly
suppress a sigh to think that our loss purchased his rest so
soon. But his great work was done ; he had told his vision,
that men might go with him to Hell, to Purgatory, and to
Heaven, and be saved from all things base. Then his weary
head was laid down in peace, and his exile was at an end.
"That fair fold in which, a lamb, he lay,"[2] was never opened
to him again, but he went home, and the blessings of the
pure in heart and strong in love go with him.

The thoughts with which we turn from the contemplation
of Dante's life and work find utterance in the lines of
Michael Angelo. "The works of Dante were unrecognised,
and his high purpose, by the ungrateful folk whose blessings
rest on all—except the just. Yet would his fate were mine !
For his drear exile, with his virtue linked, glad would I
change the fairest state on earth."

[1] *De Vulgari Eloquentia.*   [2] *Paradiso,* xxv. 5

III

HELL

THE first cantica of the "Divine Comedy"—the Inferno or Hell—is the best known of all Dante's work in prose or verse, in Latin or Italian; and though students of Dante may sometimes regret this fact, yet no one can be at a moment's loss to understand it.

For the attributes of heart and brain requisite for some kind of appreciation of the Inferno are by many degrees more common than those to which the other works of Dante appeal. It is easy to imagine a reader who has not even begun truly to understand either the poet or the poem nevertheless rendering a sincere tribute of admiration to the colossal force of the Inferno, and feeling the weird spell of fascination and horror ever tightening its grasp on him as he descends from circle to circle of that starless realm.

There is no mystery in the inveterate tendency to regard Dante as pre-eminently the poet of Hell. Nor is it a new phenomenon. Tradition tells of the women who shrank aside as Dante passed them by, and said one to another, shuddering as they spoke, "See how his black hair crisped in the fire as he passed through Hell!" But no tradition tells of awe-struck passers-by who noted that the stains had been wiped from that clear brow in Purgatory, that the gleam of that pure and dauntless eye had been kindled in Heaven.

45

The machinery of the Inferno, then, is moderately familiar to almost all. Dante, lost in the darksome forest, scared from the sunlit heights by the wild beasts that guard the mountain side, meets the shade of Virgil, sent to rescue him by Beatrice, and suffered by Omnipotence to leave for a time his abode in the limbo of the unbaptised, on this mission of redeeming love. Virgil guides Dante through the open gate of Hell, down through circle after circle of contracting span and increasing misery and sin, down to the central depth where the arch-rebel Satan champs in his triple jaws the arch-traitors against Church and State, Judas Iscariot, and Brutus and Cassius.[1]

Through all these circles Dante passes under Virgil's guidance. He sees and minutely describes the varying tortures apportioned to the varying guilt of the damned, and converses with the souls of many illustrious dead in torment.

And is this the poem that has enthralled and still enthralls so many a heart? Are we to look for the strengthening, purifying, and uplifting of our lives, are we to look for the very soul of poetry in an almost unbroken series of descriptions, unequalled in their terrible vividness, of ghastly tortures, interspersed with tales of shame, of guilt, of misery? Even so. And we shall not look in vain.

But let us listen first to Dante's own account of the subject-matter of his poem. Five words of his are better than a volume of the commentators. "The subject of the whole work, literally accepted," he says, "is the state of souls

[1] Compare pp. 15-17.

after death. . . . But if the work is taken allegorically the subject is MAN, as rendering himself liable, by good or ill desert in the exercise of his free will, to rewarding or punishing justice." [1]

According to Dante, then, the real subject of the Inferno is " Man, as rendered liable, by ill desert in the exercise of his free will, to punishing justice." Surely a subject fraught with unutterable sadness, compassed by impenetrable mystery, but one which in the hands of a prophet may well be made to yield the bread of life ; a subject fitly introduced by those few pregnant words, "The day was going, and the dusky air gave respite to the animals that are on earth from all their toils ; and I alone girt me in solitude to bear the strain both of the journey and the piteous sight, which memory that errs shall not retrace." [2]

Now if this be the true subject of the poem, it follows that all those physical horrors of which it seems almost to consist must be strictly subordinate to something else, must be part of the machinery or means by which the end of the poet is reached, but in no way the end itself.

If the subject of the poem is a moral one, then the descriptions of physical torment and horror must never even for a moment overbalance or overwhelm the true " motive" of the work, must never even for a moment so crush or deaden the feelings as to render them incapable of

1 Epistola xi. § 8.   2 *Inferno*, ii. 1-6.

moral impressions, must never in a single instance leave a prevailingly physical impression upon the mind.

And it is just herein that the transcendent power of the Inferno is displayed. Horrors which rise and ever rise in intensity till they culminate in some of the ghastliest scenes ever conceived by mortal brain are from first to last held under absolute control, are forced to support and intensify moral conceptions which in less mighty hands they would have numbed and deadened. Oh, the pity of this sin, the unutterable, indelible pity of it! Its wail can never be stilled in our hearts while thought and memory remain. The misery of some forms of sin, the foul shame of others, the vileness, the hatefulness, the hideous deformity of others yet—this, and not horror at the punishment of sin, is what Dante stamps and brands upon our hearts as we descend with him towards the central depths, stamps and brands upon our hearts till the pity, the loathing, the horror can endure no more;—then in the very depth of Hell, at the core of the Universe, with one mighty strain that leaves us well-nigh spent, we turn upon that central point, and, leaving Hell beneath our feet, ascend by the narrow path at the antipodes.

With the horror and the burden of the starless land far off, we lift up our eyes again to see the stars, and our souls are ready for the purifying sufferings of Purgatory.

Sometimes the tortures of the damned are a mere physical translation, so to speak, of their crimes. Thus the ruthless disseminators of strife and dissension who have torn asunder those who belonged one to another, those who had no proper existence apart from one another, are in their turn hewn and cleft by the avenging sword ; and ever as their bodies reunite and their wounds are healed, the fierce blow falls again. Amongst them Dante sees the great troubadour, Bertram de Born, who fostered the rebellion of the sons of our own king Henry II. In that he made father and son each other's enemy, his head is severed from his trunk, his brain from its own root.[1]

In other cases a transparent metaphor or allegory dictates the form of punishment ; as when the hypocrites crawl in utter weariness under the crushing weight of leaden garments, shaped like monkish cloaks and cowls, and all covered with shining gold outside.[2] Or when the flatterers and sycophants wallow in filth, which fitly symbolises their foul life on earth.[3]

It is probable that some special significance and appropriateness might be traced in almost all the forms of punishment in Dante's Hell, though it is not always obvious. But one thing at least is obvious : the uniform congruousness of the impression which the physical and moral factors of each description combine to produce. In fact, the Inferno is an account of " man, as deserving ill by the exercise of his free will," in which all the external surroundings are brought into precise accord with the central conception. The tortures are only the background ; and as in the picture of a great artist,

---

[1] *Inferno*, xxviii.   [2] *Ibid.* xxiii. 58 sqq.
[3] *Ibid* xviii. 103-136.

whether we can trace any special significance and appropriateness in the background or not, we always feel that it supports the true subject of the picture and never overpowers it, so it is here. Man as misusing his free will. This is the real subject of the Inferno. All else is accessory and subordinate.

But if this be so, we should expect to find an endless variety and gradation, alike of guilt and punishment, as we pass through the circles of Hell. And so we do. At one moment indignation and reproof are all swallowed up in pity, and the suffering of the exiled soul only serves to quicken an infinite compassion in our hearts, a compassion not so much for the punishment of sin as for sin itself with its woeful loss and waste of the blessings and the holiness of life. At another moment we are brought face to face with a wretch whose tortures only serve to throw his vileness into sharper relief; and when we think of him and of his deeds, of him and his victims, we can understand those awful words of Virgil's when Dante weeps, "Art thou too like the other fools? The death of pity is true pity here."[1] Infinite pity would indeed embrace the most abandoned, but it is only weak and misdirected pity that wakes or slumbers at the dictate of mere suffering.

And as there is infinite variety of guilt and woe, so is there infinite variety of character in Dante's Hell. Though the poet condemns with sternest impartiality all who have

---

[1] *Inferno*, xx. 27, 28 : 'Qui vive la pietà qand' è ben morta." The double force of pietà, "pi[e]ty," is lost in the translation.

died in unrepented sin, yet he recognises and honours the moral distinction amongst them. What a difference, for instance, between the wild blaspheming robber, Vanni Fucci,[1] and the defiant Capaneus,[2] a prototype of Milton's Satan, the one incited by the bestial rage of reckless self-abandonment, the other by the proud self-reliance of a spirit that eternity cannot break—alike in their defiance of the Almighty, but how widely severed in the sources whence it springs.

Look again where Jason strides. The wrongs he did Medea and Hypsipyle have condemned him to the fierce lash under which his base companions shriek and flee ; but he, still kingly in his mien, without a tear or cry bears his eternal pain.[3]

See Farinata, the great Florentine—in his ever burning tomb he stands erect and proud, " as holding Hell in great disdain " ; tortured less by the flames than by the thought that the faction he opposed is now triumphant in his city ; proud, even in Hell, to remember how once he stood alone between his country and destruction.[4]

See again where Pietro delle Vigne, in the ghastly forest of suicides, longs with a passionate longing that his fidelity at that time when he " held both the keys of the great Frederick's heart " should be vindicated upon earth from the unjust calumnies that drove him to self-slaughter.[5]

---

[1] *Inferno*, xxiv. 112—xxv. 9, &c. [2] *Ibid* xiv. 43-66.
[3] *Ibid.* xviii. 82-96. [4] *Ibid.* x. 22-93.
[5] *Ibid* xxiii., 55-78.

And see where statesmen and soldiers of Florence, themselves condemned for foul and unrepented sin, still love the
city in which they lived, still long to hear some good of her.
As the flakes of fire fall "like snow upon a windless day" on
their defenceless bodies, see with what dismay they gaze into
one another's eyes when Dante brings ill news to them of
Florence.[1]

In a word, the souls in Hell are what they were on earth,
no better and no worse. This is the key-note to the com-
prehension of the poem. No change has taken place; none
are made rebels to God's will, and none are brought into
submission to it, by their punishment; but all are as they
were. Even amongst the vilest there is only the rejection of
a thin disguise, no real increase of shamelessness. Many
souls desire to escape notice and to conceal their crimes, just
as they would have done on earth; many condemn their
evil deeds and are ashamed of them, just as they would have
been on earth; but there is no change of character, no in-
fusion of a new spirit either for good or ill; with all their
variety and complexity of character, the unrepentant
sinners wake in Hell, as they would wake on earth, our
mingled pity and horror, our mingled loathing and admiration. Man as misusing his free will, in all the scope and
variety of the infinite theme, is the subject of the poem.

And this brings us to another consideration: the eternity
of Dante's Hell. Those who know no other line of Dante,
know the last verse of the inscription upon the gate of Hell;

[1] *Inferno*, xvi. 64-83.

" All hope abandon, ye that enter here." The whole inscription is as follows : " Through me the way lies to the doleful city ; through me the way lies to eternal pain ; through me the way lies 'mongst the people lost. 'Twas justice moved my Lofty Maker ; Divine Power made me, Wisdom Supreme and Primal Love. Before me were no things created, save things eternal ; and I, too, last eternal. All hope abandon, ye that enter here."[1]

The gates of Hell reared by the Primal Love ! If we believe in the eternity of sin and evil, the eternity of suffering and punishment follows of necessity. To be able to acquiesce in the one, but to shrink from the thought of the other, is sheer weakness. The eternity and hopelessness of Dante's Hell are the necessary corrollaries of the impenitence of his sinners. To his mind wisdom and love cannot exist without justice, and justice demands that eternal ill-desert shall reap eternal woe.

But how could one who so well knew what an eternal Hell of sin and suffering meant, believe it to be founded on eternal love ? Why did not Dante's heart in the very strength of that eternal love rebel against the hideous belief in eternal sin and punishment ? I cannot answer the question I have asked. Dante believed in the Church, believed in the theology she taught, and could not have been what he was had he not done so. Had he rejected any of the cardinal beliefs of the Christianity of his age and rebelled against the Church, he might have been the herald of future

[1] *Inferno*, iii. 1-9.

reformations; but he could never have been the index and interpreter to remotest generations of that mediæval Catholic religion of which his poem is the very soul.

Meanwhile note this, that if ever man realised the awful mystery and contradiction involved in the conception of a good God condemning the virtuous heathen to eternal exile, that man was Dante. If ever heart of man was weighed down beneath the load of pity for the damned, that heart was Dante's. The virtuous heathen he places in the first round of Hell; here "no plaint is to be heard except of sighs, which make the eternal air to tremble"; here, with no other torture than the death of hope without the death of longing, they live in neither joy nor sorrow, eternal exiles from the realms of bliss.[1]

Dante, as we shall see hereafter, longed with a passionate thirsty longing to know how the divine justice could thus condemn the innocent. But his thirst was never slaked; it was and remained an utter mystery to him; and there are few passages of deeper pathos than those in which he remembers that his beloved and honoured guide and master, even Virgil, the very type of human wisdom and excellence, was himself amongst these outcasts.[2]

Again and again, as we pass with Dante through the circles of Hell, we feel that his yearning pity for the lost, racking his very soul and flinging him senseless to the ground for misery, shows an awakening spirit which could not long

---

[1] *Inferno*, iv. 23-45, 84.

[2] Compare e.g. *Purgatorio*, iii. 34-45, xxii. 67-73.

exist in human hearts without teaching them that God's redeeming pity is greater and more patient than their own. So, too, when Francesca and Paolo, touched by Dante's pitying sympathy, exclaim, "Oh, thou gracious being, if we were dear to God, how would we pray for thee!"[1] who can help feeling that Dante was not far from the thought that all souls are dear to God?

Meanwhile, how strong that faith which could lift up all this weight of misery and woe, and still believe in the Highest Wisdom and the Primal Love! Only the man who knew the holiness of human life to the full as well as he knew its infamy, only the man who had seen Purgatory and Heaven, and who had actually felt the love of God, could know that with all its mystery and misery the universe was made not only by the Divine Power, but by the Supreme Wisdom and the Primal Love, could weave this Trinity of Power, Wisdom, Love, into the Unity of the all-sustaining God, who made both Heaven and Hell.

And we still have to face the same insoluble mystery. The darker shade is indeed lifted from the picture upon which we gaze; we have no eternal Hell, no eternity of sin, to reckon with; but to us too comes the question, "Can the world with all its sin and misery be built indeed upon the Primal Love?" And our answer too must be the answer not of knowledge but of faith. Only by making ourselves God's fellow workers till we *feel* that the Divine power and the Primal Love are one, can we gain a faith that will sustain

[1] *Inferno*, v. 88, 91, 92.

the mystery it cannot solve.   Alas! how often our weaker
faith fails in its lighter task, how often do we speak of sin
and misery as though they were discoveries of yesterday that
had brought new trials to our faith, unknown before; how
often do we feel it hard to say even of earth what Dante in
the might of his unshaken faith could say of Hell itself—
that it is made by Power, Wisdom, Love!

But perhaps we have dwelt too long already on this topic,
and in any case we must now hasten on.   Dante's Hell, as we
have seen, represents sinful and impenitent humanity with all
its fitting surroundings and accessories, cut off from everything
that can distract the attention, confuse the moral impression,
or alleviate its appalling strength.   And as the magic power
of his words, with the absolute sincerity and clearness of his
own conceptions, forces us to realise the details of his vision
as if we had trodden every step of the way with him, this
result follows amongst others: that we realise, with a
vividness that can never again grow dim, an existence
without any one of those sweet surroundings and embellish-
ments of human life which seem the fit support and reflection
of purity and love.

We have been in a land where none of the fair sounds or
sights of nature have access, no flowers, no stars, no light, and
if there are streams and hills there they are hideously
transformed into instruments and emblems not of beauty but
of horror.   We are made to realise all this, and to feel that
it is absolutely and eternally fitting as the abode of sin and

of impenitence. And when once this association has been stamped upon our minds, the beauty and the sweetness of the world in which we live gain a new meaning for us. They become the standing protest of all that is round us against every selfish, every sinful thought or deed ; the standing appeal to us to bring our souls into sweet harmony with their surroundings, since God in His mercy brings not their surroundings into ghastly harmony with them.

When we have been with the poor wretch, deep down in Hell, who gasps in his burning fever for "the rivulets that from the green slopes of Casintino drop down into the Arno, freshening the soft, cool channels, where they glide," [1] and have realised that in that land there are not and ought not to be the cooling streams and verdant slopes of earth, we can never again enjoy the sweetness and the peace of nature without our hearts being consciously or unconsciously purified, without every evil thing in our lives feeling the rebuke.

When we have known what it is to be in a starless land, and have felt how strange and incongruous the fair sights of Heaven would be, have felt that they would have no place or meaning there, have felt that cheerless gloom alone befits the souls enveloped there, then when we leave the dreary realms and once more gaze upon the heavens by night and day, they are more to us than they have ever been before, they are indeed what Dante so often calls them, using the language of the falconers, the *lure* by which God summons back our wayward souls from vain and mean pursuits.

[1] *Inferno*, xxx. 64-67.

E

Look, again, upon this fearful picture. Dante and Virgil come to a black and muddy lake in which the passionate tear and smite one another in bestial rage; and all over its surface are bubbles rising up. They come from the cries of the morose and sullen ones "who are fixed in the slime at the bottom of the lake. They cry: 'Gloomy we were in the sweet air that the sun gladdens, bearing in our heart the smoke of sullenness; now we are gloomy here in the black slime' —such is the strain that gurgles in their throats, but cannot find full utterance." [1] Who that has seen those bubbles rise upon the lake can ever suffer himself again to cherish sullenness within his heart without feeling at the very instant the rebuke of the "sweet air that the sun gladdens," and thinking of that gurgling strain of misery?

Another of the lessons taught by the Inferno is that no plea, however moving, can avail the sinner, or take away the sinfulness of sin, that no position can place him above punishment, that no authority can shield him from it.

The guilty love of Francesco and Paolo, so strong, so deathless in that it was love, has sunk them to Hell instead of raising them to Heaven in that it was guilty. Stronger to make them one than Hell to sever them, it is powerless to redeem the sin to which it has allied itself, and its tenderness has but swelled the eternal anguish of those whom it still joins together, because it has suffered the sanctuary of life, which love is set to guard, to be polluted and betrayed.

[1] *Inferno*, vii. 117-126.

Sung in those strains of deathless tenderness and pity where "tears seem to drop from the very words," the story of this guilty love reveals the fatalest of all mischoice, and tells us that no passion, however wild in its intensity, however innocent in its beginnings, however unpremeditated in its lawless outburst, however overmastering in its pleas, however loyal to itself in time and in eternity, may dare to raise itself above the laws of God and man, or claim immunity from its wretched consequences for those who are its slaves. How infinite the pity and the waste, how irreparable the loss, when the love that might have been an ornament to Heaven, adds to the unmeasured guilt and anguish of Hell a wail of more piercing sorrow than rings through all its lower depths !

Nor could any height of place claim exemption from the moral law. Dante was a Catholic, and his reverence for the Papal Chair was deep. But against the faithless Popes he cherished a fiery indignation proportioned to his high estimate of the sacred office they abused. In one of the most fearful passages of the Inferno he describes, in terms that gain a terrible significance from one of the forms of criminal execution practised in his day, how he stood by a round hole in one of the circles of Hell, in which Pope Nicholas III. was thrust head foremost—stood like the confessor hearing the assassin's final words, and heard the guilty story of Pope Nicholas. [1]

It is characteristic of Dante that he tells us here, as if quite incidentally, that these holes were about the size of the

[1] *Inferno*, xix.

baptising stands or fonts in the Church of San Giovanni, " one
of which," says he, " I broke not many years ago to save one
who was suffocating in it. Let this suffice to disabuse all men."
Evidently he had been taxed with sacrilege for saving the
life of the dying child at the expense of the sacred vessel,
and it can hardly be an accident that he recalls this circum-
stance in the Hell of the sacrilegious Popes and Churchmen.
These men who had despied their sacred trust and turned it
to basest trafficking, were the representatives of that hard
system of soulless officialism that would pollute the holiest
functions of the Church, while reverencing with superstitious
scruple their outward symbols and instruments.

And if the Papal office could not rescue the sinner that held
it, neither could the Papal authority shield the sins of others.
It is said that Catholics have not the keeping of their own
consciences. Dante at least thought they had. In the Hell
of fraudulent counsellors, wrapped in a sheet of eternal flame
one comes to him and cries, " Grudge not to stay and speak
with me a while. Behold I grudge it not, although I burn."
It is Guido da Montefeltro, whose fame in council and in war
had gone forth to the ends of the earth. All wiles and covert
ways he knew, and there had ever been more of the fox than
of the lion in him. But when he saw himself arriving at
that age when every man should lower sails and gather in his
ropes, then did he repent of all that once had pleased him,
and girding him with the cord of St. Francis he became a
friar. Alas ! his penitence would have availed him well but
for the Prince of the new Pharisees, Pope Boniface VIII.,

who was waging war with Christians who should have been his friends, hard by the Lateran. "He demanded counsel of me," continues Guido, "but I kept silence, for his words seemed drunken. Then he said to me 'Let not thy heart misdoubt; henceforth do I absolve thee, but do thou teach me so to act that I may cast Prenestina to the ground, Heaven I can shut and open, as thou knowest.' . . . Then the weighty arguments impelled me to think silence worse than speech ; and so I said, 'Father—since thou dost cleanse me from that guilt wherein I now must fall—long promise and performance short will make thee triumph in thy lofty seat.' Then when I died St. Francis came for me, but one of the black cherubim said to him 'Do me no wrong, nor take thou him away. He must come down amongst my menials, e'en for the fraudulent advice he gave, since when I have kept close upon his hair. He who repents not cannot be absolved, nor can one will the same thing he repents, the contradiction not permitting it.' Ah wretched me ! how did I shudder then, for he laid hold of me, and with the cry 'Haply thou know'st not I was logician ?' bore me to judgment."[1]

Who can fail to recognise the utter truth of Dante's teaching here? What can stand between a man's own conscience and his duty? Though the very symbol and mouthpiece of the collective wisdom and piety of Christendom should hold the shield of authority before the culprit, yet it cannot ward off the judgment for one single deed done in

[1] *Inferno*, xxvii.

violation of personal moral conviction. When once we have
realised the meaning of this awful passage, how can we ever
urge again as an excuse for unfaithfulness to our own
consciences, that the assurance of those we loved and
reverenced overcame our scruples? Here as everywhere.
Dante strips sin of every specious and distracting circum-
stance, and shows it to us where it ought to be—in Hell.

Contrast with the scene we have just looked upon the
companion picture from the Purgatory; where Buonconte da
Montefeltro tells how he fled on foot from the battlefield of
Campaldino, his throat pierced with a mortal wound ensan-
guining the earth. Where Archiano falls into the Arno there
darkness came upon him, and he fell crossing his arms upon
his breast and calling on the name of Mary with his last
breath. "Then," he continues, "God's angel came and took
me, and Hell's angel shrieked, 'O thou of Heaven, wherefore
dost thou rob me? Thou bear'st with thee the eternal part
of him, all for one sorry tear which saves it from me. But
with the other part of him I'll deal in other fashion.'" Upon
which the infuriated demon swells the torrent with rain,
sweeps the warrior's body from the bank, dashes away the
hateful cross into which its arms are folded, and in impotent
rage rolls it along the river bed and buries it in slime so that
men never see it more; but the soul is meanwhile saved.[1]

Here we must pause. I have made no attempt to give a
systematic account of the Inferno, still less to select the
finest passages from it. I have only tried to interpret some

[1] *Purgatorio*, v. 85-129.

of the leading thoughts which run through it, some of the deep lessons which it can hardly fail to teach the reader.

Like all great works, the Inferno should be studied both in detail and as a whole in order to be rightly understood ; and when we understand it, even partially, when we have been with Dante down through all the circles to that central lake of ice in which all humanity seems frozen out of the base traitors who showed no humanity on earth, when we have faced the icy breath of the eternal air winnowed by Satan's wings, and have been numbed to every thought and feeling except one—one which has been burned and frozen into our hearts through all those rounds of shame and woe—the thought of the pity, the misery, the hatefulness of sin ; then, but then only, we shall be ready to understand the Purgatory, shall know something of what the last lines of the Inferno meant to Dante; "We mounted up, he first and second I until through a round opening I saw some of those beauteous things that Heaven bears ; and thence we issued forth again to see the stars." [1]

1 *Inferno* xxxiv. 136-139.

IV.

PURGATORY

"LEAVING behind her that so cruel sea, the bark of poesy now spreads her sails to speed o'er happier waters; and I sing of that mid kingdom where the soul of man is freed from stain, till worthy to ascend to Heaven."[1] Such are the opening words of Dante's Purgatory, and they drop like balm upon our seared and wounded hearts when we have escaped from the dread abode of eternal ill-desert.

"Man, atoning for the misuse of his free will," may be regarded as the subject of this poem. And it brings it, in a sense, nearer to us than either the Hell or the Paradise. Perhaps it ought not to surprise us that the Purgatory has not by any means taken such a hold of the general imagination as the Hell, and that its machinery and incidents are therefore far less widely known; for the power of the Purgatory does not overwhelm us, whether we understand or no, like that of the Inferno. There are passages indeed in the poem, which take the reader by storm, and force themselves upon his memory, but as a rule it must be felt in its deeper spiritual meaning to be felt at all. Its gentleness is ultimately as strong as the relentless might of the Hell, but it works more slowly and takes time to sink into our hearts and diffuse its influence there. Nor again need we be surprised that the inner circle of Dante students often

[1] *Purgatorio*, i. 1-6.

oncentrate their fullest attention and admiration upon the Paradise, for it is the Paradise in which the poet is most absolutely unique and unapproached, and in it his admirers rightly find the supreme expression of his spirit.

And yet there is much in the Purgatory that seems to render it peculiarly fitted to support our spiritual life and help us in our daily conflict, much which we might reasonably have expected would give its images and allegories a permanent place in the devout heart of Christendom; for, as already hinted, it is nearer to us in our struggles and imperfections, in our aspirations and our conscious unworthiness, nearer to us in our love of purity and our knowledge that our own hearts are stained with sin, in our desire for the fulness of God's light, and our knowledge that we are not yet worthy or ready to receive it; it is nearer to us in its piercing appeals, driven home to the moral experience of every day and hour, nearer to us in its mingled longing and resignation, in its mingled consolations and sufferings, nearer to us in its deep unrest of unattained but unrelinquished ideals, than either the Hell in its ghastly harmony of impenitence and suffering, or the Paradise in its ineffable fruition.

Moreover, the allegorical appropriateness of the various punishments is far more obvious and simple, and the spiritual significance of the whole machinery clearer and more direct, in the Purgatory than in the Hell. In a word, the Purgatory is more obviously though not more truly, more directly though not more profoundly, moral and spiritual in its purport than the Hell.

Dante addresses some of the sufferers on the fifth circle of Purgatory as " chosen ones of God whose pains are soothed by justice and by hope."[1] And in truth the spirits in Purgatory are already utterly separated from their sins in heart and purpose, are already chosen ones of God. They are deeply sensible of the justice of their punishment, and they are fed by the certain hope that at last, when purifying pain has done its work, their past sins will no longer separate them from God, they will not only be parted in sympathy and emotion from their own sinful past, but will be so cut off from it as no longer to feel it as their own, no longer to recognise it as part of themselves, no longer to be weighed down by it. Then they will rise away from it into God's presence. " Repenting and forgiving," says one of them, "we passed from life, at peace with God, who pierces our hearts with longing to see Him."[2]

The souls in Purgatory, then, are already transformed by the thirst for the living water, already filled with the longing to see God, already at one with Him in will, already gladdened by the hope of entering into full communion with Him. But they do not wish to go into His presence yet. The sense of shame and the sense of justice forbid it. They feel that the unexpiated stains of former sins still cleave to them, making them unfit for Heaven, and they love the purifying torments which are burning those stains away. In the topmost circle of Purgatory amongst the fierce flames from which Dante would have hurled himself into molten

[1] *Purgatorio*, xix, 76 sqq.   [2] *Ibid.* v. 55-57.

glass for coolness, he sees souls whose cheeks flush at the memory of their sin with a shame that adds a burning to the burning flame ; whilst others clustering at the edge that they may speak with him yet take good heed to keep within the flame, lest for one moment they should have respite from the fierce pain which is purging away their sins and drawing them nearer to their desire.[1]

Sweet hymns of praise and supplication are the fitting solace of this purifying pain ; and as Dante passes through the first of the narrow ascents that lead from circle to circle of Purgatory, he may well contrast this place of torment with the one that he has left, may well exclaim, " Ah me ! how diverse are these straits from those of Hell ! "[2]

Penitence, humility, and peace—though not the highest or the fullest peace—are the key-notes of the Purgatory.

When Dante issued from the deadly shades of Hell, his cheeks all stained with tears, his eyes and heart heavy with woe, his whole frame spent with weariness and agony, the sweet blue heavens stretched above him, and his eyes, that for so long had gazed on nought but horror, rested in their peaceful depths ; Venus, the morning star, brightened the east, and the Southern Cross poured its splendour over the heavens ; daybreak was at hand, and the poets were at the foot of the mount of Purgatory.

The melting hoar frost, when the sun rose, served to

[1] *Purgatorio*, xxvi. 13-15, 81 : xxvii. 49-51.
[2] *Purgatorio*, xii. 112, 113.

bathe away the stains and tears of Hell from Dante's cheeks. The sea rippled against the mountain ; and reeds, the emblems of humility, ever yielding to the wave that swept them, clustered round the shore.

Ere long the waves were skimmed by a light bark, a radiant angel standing in the prow, bearing the souls of the redeemed, who must yet be purified, singing the psalm, " When Israel came out of Egypt." Amongst the shades thus borne to the mount of purification was Dante's friend Casella, the singer and musician. How often had his voice lulled all Dante's cares to sleep, and "quieted all his desires," and now it seemed as though he were come to bring his troubled heart to peace, to rest him in his utter weariness of body and of soul.

So, at his entreaty, Casella raised his voice, and all the shades gathered entranced around him as he sang a noble canzone composed by Dante himself in years gone by.[1] The sweet sound never ceased to echo in the poet's memory—not even the ineffable harmonies of Paradise drowned those first strains of peace that soothed him after his awful toil.

But Purgatory is no place of rest, and Casella's song was rudely interrupted by the guardian of the place, who cried aloud, " How now, ye sluggard souls ! What negligence and what delay is here ? Speed to the mountain ! Rid you of the crust that lets not God be manifest to you ! " To purge our sins away is not to rest ; and no longing for repose must tempt us to delay even for a moment.[2]

[1] Canzone xv. " Amor, che nella mente." See also *Convito*, trat. iii.
[2] *Purgatorio*, i,

Dante draws no flattering picture of the ease of purification ; Hell itself hardly gives us such a sense of utter
weariness as the first ascent of the mount of Purgatory.
Virgil is on in front, and Dante cries out, altogether spent,
" O, my sweet father, turn thee and behold how I am left
alone unless thou stay " ; but Virgil urges him on, and after
a time comforts him with the assurance that though the
mountain is so hard to scale at first, yet the higher a man
climbs the easier the ascent becomes, till at last it is so sweet
and easy to him that he rises without effort as a boat drops
down the stream : then he may know that the end of his
long journey has come, that the weight of sin is cast off,
that his soul obeys its own pure nature, and rises
unencumbered to its God.[1]

The lower portion of the mountain forms a kind of
ante-Purgatory, where the souls in weary exile wait for
admission to the purifying pain for which they long.   Here
those who have delayed their penitence till the end of life
atone for their wilful alienation by an equal term of forced
delay ere they may enter the blessed suffering of Purgatory.
Here those who have died in contumacy against the Church
expiate their offences by a thirty-fold exile in the ante-
Purgatory ; but as we saw in Hell that Papal absolution will
not shield the sinful soul, so we find in Purgatory that the
Papal malediction, the thunders of excommunication itself,
cannot permanently part the repentant soul from the
forgiving God.[2]

[1] *Purgatorio*, iv. 37-95.   [2] *Ibid.* iii. 112-145, iv. 127-135.

When this first exile is at an end, and the lower mountain scaled, the gate of the true Purgatory is reached. Three steps lead up to it, "the first of marble white, so polished and so smooth that in it man beholds him as he is." This represents that transparent simplicity and sincerity of purpose that, throwing off all self-delusion, sees itself as it is and is the first step towards true penitence. "The second step, darker than purpled black, of rough and calcined stone, all rent through length and breadth," represents the contrite heart of true affliction for past sin. "The third and crowning mass methought was porphyry, and flamed like the red blood fresh spouting from the vein." This is the glowing love which crowns the work of penitence, and gives the earnest of a new and purer life. Above these steps an angel stands to whom Peter gave the keys—the silver key of knowledge and the golden key of authority—bidding him open to the penitent, and err rather towards freedom than towards over-sternness.[1]

Within the gate of Purgatory rise the seven terraces where sin is purged. On the three lower ledges man atones for that perverse and ill-directed love which seeks another's ill—for love of some sort is the one sole motive of all action, good or bad.[2] In the lowest circle the pride that rejoices in its own superiority, and therefore in the inferiority of others, is purged and expiated. "As to support a ceiling or a roof,"

[1] *Purgatorio*, ix. 76-129.
[2] For the general scheme of Purgatory, see *Purgatorio*, xvii. 91-139.

says Dante, "one sees a figure bracket-wise with knees bent up against its bosom, till the imaged strain begets real misery in him who sees, so I beheld those shades when close I scanned them. True it is that less or greater burdens cramped each one or less or more, yet he whose mien had most of patience, wailing seemed to say, 'I can no more!'" [1]

In the second circle the blind sin of envy is expiated. Here the eyelids of the envious are ruthlessly pierced and closed by the stitch of an iron wire and through the horrid suture gush forth tears of penitence that bathe the sinner's cheeks. "Here shall my eyes be closed," says Dante, half in shame at seeing those who saw him not, "here shall my eyes be closed, though open now—but not for long. Far more I dread the pain of those below; for even now methinks I bend beneath the load." [2]

In the third circle the passionate wend their way through a blinding, stinging smoke, darker than Hell; but all are one in heart and join in sweet accord of strain and measure singing the "Agnus Dei."

In these three lower circles is expiated the perverse love that, in pride, in envy, or in passion, seeks another's ill.

Round the fourth or central ledge hurry in ceaseless flight the laggards whose feeble love of God, though not perverse, was yet inadequate.

Then on the succeeding circles are punished those whose sin was excessive, and ill-regulated love of earthly things.

[1] *Purgatorio* x. 130-139.
[2] *Ibid.* xiii. 73, 74, 133-138.

There in the fifth round the avaricious and the prodigal, who alike bent their thoughts to the gross things of earth and lost all power of good, lie with their faces in the dust and their backs turned to heaven, pinioned and helpless.

In the sixth circle the gluttonous in lean and ghastly hunger gaze from hollow eyes "like rings without the gems," upon the fruit they may not taste. [1]

And lastly in the seventh circle the sin of unchastity is purged, in flames as fierce as its own reckless passion.

Through all of these circles to which its life on earth has rendered it liable, the soul must pass, in pain but not in misery; at perfect peace with God, loving the pain that makes it fit to rise into His presence, longing for that more perfect union, but not desiring it as yet because still knowing itself unworthy.

At last the moment comes when this shrinking from God's presence, this clinging to the pain of Purgatory, has its end. The desire to rise up surprises the repentant soul, and that desire is itself the proof that the punishment is over, that the soul is ripe for Heaven. Then, as it ascends, the whole mountain shakes from base to summit with the mighty cry of " Gloria in excelsis ! " raised by every soul in Purgatory as the ransomed and emancipated spirit seeks its home. [2]

Through all these circles Dante is led by Virgil, and here as in Hell he meets and converses with spirits of the departed. He displays the same unrivalled power and the same relentless

[1] *Purgatorio*, xxiii. 31.
[2] *Purgatorio*, xx. 124-151, xxi. 34-78.

use of it, the same passionate indignation, the same yearning pity, which take the soul captive in the earlier poem. In the description of Corso Donati's charger dragging his mangled body towards the gorge of Hell in ever fiercer flight; in the indignant protest against the factious spirit of Italy and the passionate appeal to the Empire; in the description of the impotent rage of the fiend who is cheated of the soul of Buonconte by "one sorry tear"; in the scathing denunciations of the cities of the Arno; [1] in these and in many another passage the poet of the Purgatory shows that he is still the poet of the Hell; but it is rather to the richness of the new thoughts and feelings than to the unabated vigour and passion of the old ones, that we naturally direct our attention in speaking of the Purgatory. And these we have by no means exhausted.

When Dante first entered the gate of Purgatory he heard "voices mingled with sweet strains" chanting the Te Deum, and they raised in his heart such images as when we hear voices singing to the organ and "partly catch and partly miss the words."[2] And this sweet music, only to find its fullest and distinctest utterance in the Paradise, pervades almost the whole of the Purgatory, filling it with a reposeful longing that prepares for the fruition it does not give.

There is a tender and touching simplicity in the records of their earthly lives which the gentle souls in Purgatory give to our poet. Take as an example the story of Pope Adrian V.,

---

1 *Purgatorio*, xxiv. 82-87, vi. 76-151, v. 85-129, xiv. 16-72.
2 *Ibid.* ix. 139-145.

whom Dante finds amongst the avaricious : " A month and little more I felt the weight with which the Papal mantle presses on his shoulders who would keep it from the mire. All other burdens seem like feathers to it. Ah me! but late was my conversion ; yet when I became Rome's Shepherd then I saw the hollow cozenage of life ; for my heart found no repose in that high dignity, and yonder life on earth gave it no room to aim yet higher: wherefore the love of this life rose within me. Till then was I a wretched soul severed from God, enslaved to avarice, for which thou seest I now bear the pain." [1]

Most touching too are the entreaties of the souls in Purgatory for the prayers of those on earth, or their confession that they have already been lifted up by them. " Tell my Giovanna to cry for me where the innocent are heard," says Nino to Dante ; [2] and when the poet meets his friend Forese, who had been dead but five years, in the highest circle but one of Purgatory, whereas he would have expected him still to be in exile at the mountain's base, he asks him to explain the reason why he is there, and Forese answers, "It is my Nella's broken sobs that have brought me so soon to drink the sweet wormwood of torment. Her devout prayers and sighs have drawn me from the place of lingering, and freed me from the lower circles. My little widow, whom I greatly loved, is all the dearer and more pleasing to God because her goodness stands alone amid surrounding vice."

[1] *Purgatorio*, xix. 103-114.
[2] *Purgatorio*, viii. 71, 72.   [3] *Ibid.* xxiii. 85-93.

Surely it is a deep and holy truth, under whatever
varying forms succeeding ages may embody it, that the
faithful love of a pure soul does more than any other earthly
power to hasten the passage of the penitent through Purgatory. When under the load of self-reproach and shame that
weighs down our souls, we dare not look up to Heaven, dare
not look into our own hearts, dare not meet God, then the
faithful love of a pure soul can raise us up and teach us not
to despair of ourselves, can lift us on the wings of its prayer,
can waft us on the breath of its sobs, swiftly through the
purifying anguish into the blissful presence of God.

A feature of special beauty in the Purgatory is formed by
the allegorical or typical sculptures on the wall and floor of
one of the terraces, by the voices of warning or encourage-
ment that sweep round the mountain, and by the visions
that from time to time visit the poet himself. Let one of
these visions suffice. Dante is about to enter the circles in
which the inordinate love of earthly things, with all vain and
vicious indulgence, is punished. "In dream there came to
me," he says, "a woman with a stuttering tongue, and with
distorted eyes, all twisted on her feet, maimed in her hands,
and sallow in her hue. I gazed at her, and as the sun
comforts the chilled limbs by the night oppressed, so did my
look give ease unto her speech, and straightway righted her
in every limb, and with love's colours touched her haggard
face. And when her speech was liberated thus, she sang so
sweetly that 'twere dire pain to wrest attention from her.

'I,' she sang, 'am that sweet siren who led astray the sailors in mid-sea, so full am I of sweetness to the ear. 'Twas I that drew Ulysses from his way with longing for my song ! and he on whom the custom of my voice has grown, full rarely leaves me, so do I content him.'" In the end this false siren is exposed in all her foulness, and Dante turns from her in loathing.[1]

Throughout Purgatory Dante is still led and instructed by Virgil. I think there is nothing in the whole Comedy so pathetic as the passages in which the fate of Virgil, to be cut off for ever from the light of God, is contrasted with the hope of the souls in Purgatory. The sweetness and beauty of Virgil's character as conceived by Dante grow steadily upon us throughout this poem, until they make the contemplation of his fate and the patient sadness with which he speaks of it more heartrending than anything that we have heard or seen in Hell. After this we hardly need to hear from Dante the direct expression he subsequently gives of his passionate thirst to know the meaning of so mysterious a decree as that which barred Heaven against the unbaptised.

In Purgatory, Virgil and Dante meet the emancipated soul of the Roman poet Statius, freed at last after many centuries of purifying pain, and ready now to ascend to Heaven. Virgil asks him how he became a Christian, and Statius refers him to his own words in one of the Eclogues, regarded in those days as containing a prophecy of Christ. "Thou," says Statius, "didst first guide me to Parnassus to

[1] *Purgatorio*, xix. 7-33.

drink in its grottoes, and afterward thou first didst light me unto God. When thou didst sing, 'The season is renewed, justice returns, and the first age of man, and a new progeny descends from Heaven,' thou wast as one who, marching through the darkness of the night, carries the light behind him, aiding not himself, but teaching those who follow him the way. Through thee was I a poet, and through thee a Christian." Not a shade of envy, not a thought of resentment or rebellion, passes over Virgil's heart as he hears that while saving others he could not save himself.[1]

But now without dwelling further on the episodes of the poem, we must hasten to consider the most beautiful and profoundest of its closing scenes.

Under Virgil's guidance Dante had traversed all the successive circles of the mount of Purgatory. He stood at its summit, in the earthly Paradise, the Garden of Eden which Eve had lost. There amid fairest sights and sounds he was to meet the glorified Beatrice, and she was to be his guide in Heaven as Virgil had been his guide in Hell and Purgatory.

In any degree to understand what follows we must try to realise the intimate blending of lofty abstract conceptions and passionate personal emotions and reminiscences in Dante's thoughts of Beatrice.

This sweet and gentle type of womanhood, round whose earthly life the genius and devotion of Dante have twined a wreath of the tenderest poetry, the most romantic love that

<hr />

[1] *Purgatorio,* xxii. 55-73.

ever rose from the heart of man, had been to him in life and death the vehicle and messenger of God's highest grace. Round her memory clustered all the noblest purposes and purest motives of his life, and in her spirit seemed to be reflected the divenest truth, the loftiest wisdom, that the human soul could comprehend. And so, making her objectively and in the scheme of the universe what she had really been and was to him subjectively, he came to regard her as the symbol of Divine philosophy as Virgil was the symbol of human virtue and wisdom.

Touched by the glow of an ideal love, Dante had reached a deeper knowledge, a fuller grace, than the wisdom of this world could teach or gain. The doctors of the Church, the sweet singers, the mighty heroes, the profound philosophers, who had instructed and supported him, had none of them touched his life so deeply, had none of them led him so far into the secret place of truth, had none of them brought him so near to God, as that sweet child, that lovely maid, that pure woman, who had given him his first and noblest ideal.

Now to Dante and to his age it was far from unnatural to erect concrete human beings into abstract types or personifications. Leah and Rachel are the active and the contemplative life respectively. Virgil, we have seen, is human philosophy. Cato of Utica represents the triumph over the carnal nature and the passions. Why should the Old Testament and classical antiquity alone furnish these types? Why should not Beatrice become the personification of that heavenly wisdom, that true knowledge of God, of which she had been the vehicle to Dante?

But to the poet and to the age in which he lived it was impossible to separate this heavenly wisdom in its simple, spiritual essence, from the form which its exposition had received at the hands of the great teachers of the Church. To them true spiritual wisdom, personal experience and knowledge of God, were inseparable from *theology*. The two united in the conception of Divine philosophy. Thus by a strange but intelligible gradation Dante blended in his conception of Beatrice two elements which seem to us the very extreme of incompatibility. She is in the first place the personification of scholastic theology, with all its subtle intricacy of pedantic method; she is in the second place the maiden to whom Dante sang his songs of love in Florence, and whose early death he wept disconsolate. And in the closing scenes of the Purgatory these two conceptions are more intimately blended, perhaps, than anywhere else in Dante's writings.

After wandering, as it were, in the forest of a bewildered life, the poet is led through Hell and Purgatory until he stands face to face at last with his own purest and loftiest ideal; and the fierceness of his own self-accusation when thus confronted with Beatrice he expresses under the form of reproaches which he lays upon *her* lips, but which we must retranslate into the reproachful utterances of his own tortured heart, if we are to retain our gentle thoughts of Beatrice.

We need not dwell even for a moment on the gorgeous pageantry with which Dante introduces and surrounds

Beatrice. Suffice it to say that she comes in a mystic car, which represents the Church, surrounded by saints and angels.

No sooner does Dante see her, although closely veiled, than the might of the old passion sweeps upon him, and like a child that flees in terror to its mother, so does he turn to Virgil with the cry : "Not one drop of blood but trembles in my veins ! I recognise the tokens of the ancient flame." But Virgil is gone. Dante has no refuge from his own offended and reproachful ideal. As he bursts into lamentations at the loss of Virgil's companionship, Beatrice sternly calls him back : "Dante! weep not that Virgil has gone from thee. Thou hast a deeper wound for which to weep."

As one who speaks, but holds back words more burning than he utters, so she stood. A clear stream flowed between her and Dante, and as she began to renew her reproaches he cast down his eyes in shame upon the water ;—but there he saw himself ! The angels sang a plaintive psalm, and Dante knew that they were pleading for him more clearly than if they had used directer words. Then the agony of shame and penitence that Beatrice's reproof had frozen in his bosom, as when the icy north wind freezes the snow amid the forests of the Apennine, was melted by the angel's plea for him as snow by the breezes of the south, and burst from him in a convulsion of sobs and tears.

How was it possible that he should have gone so far astray, have been so false to the promise and the purpose of his early life, have abused his own natural gifts and the superadded grace of heaven ? How was it possible that he should have let all the richness of his life run wild? That after Beatrice had for a time sustained him and led him in the true path with her sweet eyes, he should have turned away from her in Heaven whom he had so loved on earth? How could he have followed the false semblances of good that never hold their word? His visions and his dreams of the ideal he was deserting had not sufficed, and so deep had he sunk, that nothing short of visiting the region of the damned could save him from perdition. Why had he deserted his first purposes? What obstacle had baffled or appalled him? What new charm had those lower things of earth obtained to draw him to them? "The false enticements of the present things," he sobbed, " had led his feet aside, soon as her countenance was hid." But should not the decay of that fair form have been itself the means of weaning him from things of earth, that he might ne'er again be cheated by their beauty or drawn aside by them from the pursuit of heavenly wisdom and of heavenly love? When the fairest of all earthly things was mouldering in the dust, should he not have freed himself from the entanglements of the less beauteous things remaining?

To all these reproaches, urged by Beatrice, Dante had no reply. With eyes rooted to the ground, filled with unutterable shame, like a child repentant and confessing, longing to throw himself at his mother's feet, but afraid to meet her glance while her lips still utter the reproof, so Dante stood. From time to time a few broken words, which needed the eye more than the ear to interpret them, dropped from his lips like shafts from a bow that breaks with excess of strain as the arrow is discharged.

At last Beatrice commanded him to look up. The wind uproots the oak tree with less resistance than Dante felt ere he could turn his downcast face to hers; but when he saw her, transcending her former self more than her former self transcended others, his agony of self-reproach and penitence was more than he could bear, and he fell senseless to the ground.[1]

When he awoke he was already plunged in the waters of Lethe, which with the companion stream of Eunoë would wash from his memory the shame and misery of past unfaithfulness, would enable him, no longer crushed by self-reproach, to ascend with the divine wisdom and purity of his own ideal into the higher realms.

And here the Purgatory ends, the Paradise begins.

[1] *Purgatorio,* xxx. 22—xxxi. 90.

V

HEAVEN

WHEN Dante wrote the Paradise, he well knew that he was engaged in the supreme effort of his life, to which all else had led up. He well knew that he was engaged in no pastime, but with intense concentration of mature power was delivering such a message from God to man as few indeed had ever been privileged or burdened to receive. He well knew that the words in which through years of toil he had distilled the sweetness and the might of his vision were immortal, that to latest ages they would bear strength and purity of life, would teach the keen eye of the spirit to gaze into the uncreated light, and would flood the soul with a joy deeper than all unrest or sorrow, with a glory that no gloom could ever dispel. He knew moreover that this his last and greatest poem would speak to a few only in any generation, though speaking to those few with a voice of transforming power and grace.

"O, ye," he cries almost at the beginning of the Paradise, "who, desirous to hear, have followed in light bark behind my keel, which sings upon its course, now turn you back and make for your own shores, trust not the open wave lest, losing me, ye should be left bewildered. As yet all untracked is the wave I sail. Minerva breathes, Apollo leads me on, and the nine Muses point me to the pole. Ye other few,

who timely have lift up your heads for bread of angels, fed
by which man liveth but can never surfeit know, well may
ye launch upon the ocean deep, keeping my furrow as ye cut
your way through waters that return and equal lie."[1]

In these last words, comparing the track he leaves to the
watery furrow that at once subsides, Dante seems to indicate
that he was well aware how easily the soul might drop out
of his verses, how the things he had to say were essentially
unutterable, so that his words could at best only be a
suggestion of his meaning dependent for their effect upon
the subtlest spiritual influences and adjustments, as well as
upon the receptive sympathy of those to whom they were
addressed. And if there are so many that fail to catch the
spirit and feel the heavenly harmony of the music when it
is Dante's own hand that touches the strings, how hopeless
seems the task of transferring even its echo, by translated
extracts, or descriptions, from which the soul has fled.

There is indeed much that is beautiful, much that is
profound, in the Paradise, which is capable of easy repro-
duction, but the divine aroma of the whole could only be
translated or transferred by another Dante. Petal after
petal of the rose of Paradise may be described or copied,
but the heavenly perfume that they breathe is gone.

"His glory that moves all things," so Dante begins the
Paradise, "pierces the universe; and is here more, here less
resplendent. In that Heaven which of His light has most,
was I. There I saw things which he who thence descends

1 *Paradiso*, ii. 1-15.

has not the knowledge or power to retell. For as it draws anigh to its desire, our intellect pierces so deep that memory cannot follow in its track. But of that sacred empire so much as I had power in my mind to store, shall now be matter of my poesy."[1]

And again, almost at the close he sings, "As he who dreams, and when the dream is broke still feels the emotion stamped upon his heart though all he saw is fled beyond recall, e'en such am I; for, all the vision gone well-nigh without a trace, yet does the sweetness that was born of it still drop within my heart."[2]

If so much as an echo of that echo, if so much as a dream of that dream, falls upon our ears and sinks into our hearts, then we are amongst those few for whom Dante wrote his last and his divinest poem.

Through the successive heavens of Paradise Dante is conducted by Beatrice; and here again the intimate blending in the divine guide of two distinct almost contradictory conceptions forms one of the great obstacles toward giving an intelligible account of the poem. This obstacle can only disappear when patient study guided by receptive sympathy has led us truly into the poet's thought.

In the Paradise, however, the allegorical and abstract element in the conception of Beatrice is generally the ruling one. She is the impersonation of Divine Philosophy, under

[1] *Paradiso*, i. 1-12.
[2] *Ibid.* xxxiii. 58-63.

whose guidance the spiritual discernment is so quickened and the moral perceptions so purified, that the intellect can thread its way through subtlest intricacies of casuistry and theology, and where the intellect fails the eye of faith still sees.

Even in this allegorical character Beatrice is a veritable personality, as are Lucia, the Divine Grace, and other attributes or agents of the Deity, who appear in the Comedy as personal beings with personal affections and feelings, though at the same time representing abstract ideas. Thus Beatrice, as Divine Philosophy impersonated, is at once an abstraction and a personality. "The eyes of Philosophy," says Dante elsewhere, "are her demonstrations, the smile of Philosophy her persuasions."[1] And this mystic significance must never be lost sight of when we read of Beatrice's eyes kindling with an ever brighter glow and her smile beaming through them with a diviner sweetness as she ascends through heaven after heaven ever nearer to the presence of God. The demonstrations of Divine Philosophy become more piercing, more joyous, more triumphant, her persuasions more soul-subduing and entrancing, as the spirit draws nearer to its source.

But though we shall never understand the Paradise unless we perceive the allegorical significance and appropriateness not only of the general conception of Beatrice, but also of many details in Dante's descriptions of her, yet we should be equally far from the truth if we imagined her a mere

[1] *Convito*, III. xv.

allegory. She is a glorified and as it were divine *personality*, and watches over and guides her pupil with the tenderness and love of a gentle and patient mother. The poet constantly likens himself to a wayward, a delirious, or a frightened child, as he flies for refuge to his blessed guide's maternal care.[1]

Again, they are in the eighth heaven, and Beatrice knows that a manifestation of saints and angels is soon to be vouchsafed to Dante. Listen to his description of her as she stands waiting; " E'en as a bird amongst the leaves she loves, brooding upon the nest of her sweet young throughout the night wherein all things are hid, foreruns the time to see their loved aspect and find them food, wherein her heavy toil is sweet to her, there on the open spray, waiting with yearning longing for the sun, fixedly gazing till the morn shall rise; so did she stand erect, her eyes intent upon the region of the solstice. And seeing her suspended in such longing I became as one who yearns for what he knows not, and who rests in hope."[2]

Under Beatrice's guidance, then, Dante ascends through the nine heavens into the empyrean heights of Paradise. Here in reality are the souls of all the blessed, rejoicing in the immediate presence and light of God,[3] and here Dante sees them in the glorified forms which they will wear after

---

[1] *Purgatorio*, xxx. 79-81, xxxi. 64-67: *Paradiso*, i. 100-102. xxii. 1 sqq.

[2] *Paradiso*, xxiii. 1-15.   [3] *Ibid*. iv. 28-48.

the resurrection. But in order to bring home to his human understanding the varied grades of merit and beatitude in Paradise, he meets or appears to meet the souls of the departed in the successive heavens through which he passes, sweeping with the spheres in wider and ever wider arc, as he rises towards the eternal rest by which all other things are moved.

It is in these successive heavens that Dante converses with the souls of the blessed. In the lower spheres they appear to him in a kind of faint bodily form like the reflections cast by glass unsilvered ; but in the higher spheres they are like gems of glowing light, like stars that blaze into sight or fade away in the depths of the sky; and these living topaz and ruby lights, like the morning stars that sing together in Job, break into strains of ineffable praise and joy as they glow upon their way in rhythmic measure both of voice and movement.

Thus in the fourth Heaven, the Heaven of the Sun, Dante meets the souls of the great doctors of the Church. Thomas Aquinas is there, and Albertus Magnus and the Venerable Bede and many more. A circle of these glorious lights is shining round Dante and Beatrice as Aquinas tells the poet who they were on earth. "Then like the horologue, that summons us, what hour the spouse of God rises to sing her matins to her spouse, to win his love, wherein each part urges and draws its fellow, making a tinkling sound of so sweet note that the well-ordered spirit swells with love ; so did I see the glorious wheel revolve, and render voice to voice in melody and sweetness such as ne'er could noted be save where rejoicing is eternalised.

"Oh, senseless care of mortals! Ah, how false the thoughts that urge thee in thy downward flight! One was pursuing law, and medicine one, one hunting after priesthood, and a fourth would rule by force or fraud; one toiled in robbery, and one in civil business, and a third was moiling in the pleasures of the flesh all surfeit-weary, and a fourth surrendered him to sloth. And I the while, released from all these things, thus gloriously with Beatrice was received in heaven."[1]

When Beatrice fixes her eyes—remember their allegorical significance as the demonstrations of Divine philosophy—upon the light of God, and Dante gazes upon them, then quick as thought and without sense of motion, the two arise into a higher heaven, like the arrow that finds its mark while yet the bow string trembles; and Dante knows by the kindling beauty that glows in his guardian's eyes that they are nearer to the presence of God and are sweeping Heaven in a wider arc.

The spirits in the higher heavens see God with clearer vision, and therefore love Him with more burning love, and rejoice with a fuller joy in His presence than those in the lower spheres. Yet these too rest in perfect peace and oneness with God's will.

In the Heaven of the Moon, for instance, the lowest of all, Dante meets Piccarda. She was the sister of Forese,

[1] *Paradiso*, x. 139—xi. 12.

whom we saw in the highest circle but one of Purgatory, raised so far by his widowed Nella's prayers. When Dante recognises her amongst her companions, in her transfigured beauty, he says, " 'But tell me, ye whose blessedness is here, do ye desire a more lofty place, to see more and to be more loved by God?' She with those other shades first gently smiled, then answered me so joyous that she seemed to glow with love's first flame, 'Brother, the power of love so lulls our will, it makes us long for nought but what we have, and feel no other thirst. If we should wish to be exalted more, our wish would be discordant with His will who here assigned us; and that may not be within these spheres, as thou thyself mayst see, knowing that here we needs must dwell in love, and thinking what love is. Nay, 'tis inherent in this blessedness to hold ourselves within the will Divine, whereby our wills are one. That we should be thus rank by rank throughout this realm ordained, rejoices all the realm e'en as its King, who draws our wills in His. And His decree is our peace. It is that sea to which all things are moved which it creates and all that nature forges.' Then was it clear to me how everywhere in Heaven is Paradise, e'en though the grace distil not in one mode from that Chief Good."[1]

So again in the second heaven, the Heaven of Mercury, the soul of Justinian tells the poet how that sphere is assigned to them whose lofty aims on earth were in some measure fed by love of fame and glory rather than inspired by the true

---

[1] *Paradiso*, iii. 64-90.

love of God. Hence they are in this lower sphere. Yet
part of their very joy consists in measuring the exact accord
between the merits and the blessedness of the beatified.
"As diverse voices make sweet melody," he continues, "so do
the diverse ranks of our life render sweet harmony amidst
these spheres." [1]

Indeed, one of the marvels of this marvellous poem is
the extreme variety of character and even of incident which
we find in Heaven as well as in Hell and Purgatory. In
each of the three poems there is one key-note to which we
are ever brought back, but in each there is infinite variety
and delicacy of individual delineation too. The saints are
no more uniform and characterless in their blessedness than
are the unrepentant sinners in their tortures or the repentant
in their contented pain.

Nor must we suppose that the Paradise is an unbroken
succession of descriptions of heavenly bliss. Here, too, as
in Hell and Purgatory, the things of earth are from time
to time discussed by Dante and the spirits that he meets.
Here too the glow of a lofty indignation flushes the very
spheres of Heaven. Thus Peter cries against Pope Boniface
VIII.: "He who usurps upon the earth my place, *my place*,
MY· PLACE, which in the presence of the Son of God is vacant
now, has made the city of my sepulture a sink of blood and
filth, at which the rebel Satan, who erst fell from Heaven
rejoices down in Hell." And at this the whole Heaven glows
with red, and Beatrice's cheek flushes as at a tale of shame. [2]

[1] *Paradiso*, vi. 112-126.   [2] *Paradiso*, xxvii. 22-34.

Dante is still the same. The sluggish self-indulgence of the monks, the reckless and selfish ambition of the factious nobles and rulers, the venial infamy of the Court of Rome cannot be banished from his mind even by the beatific visions of Heaven. Nay, the very contrast gives a depth of indignant sadness to the denunciations of the Paradise which makes them almost more terrible than those of Hell itself. Interwoven too with the descriptions of the bliss of Heaven, is the discussion of so wide a range of moral and theological topics that the Paradise has been described as having "summed up, as it were, and embodied for perpetuity . . . the quintessence, the living substance, the ultimate conclusions of the scholastic theology;"[1] and it may well be true that to master the last cantica of the "Divine Comedy" is to pierce more deeply into the heart of mediæval religion and theology than any of the schoolmen and doctors of the Church can take us. At the touch of Dante's staff, the flintiest rock of metaphysical dogma yields the water of life, and in his hands the subtlest discussion of casuistry becomes a lamp to our feet.

And beyond all this, such is the marvellous concentration of Dante's poetry, there is room in the Paradise for long digressions, biographical, antiquarian, and personal; whilst all these parts, apparently so heterogeneous, are welded into perfect symmetry in this one poem.

Amongst the most important of the episodes is the account of ancient Florence given to Dante by his ancestor Cacciaguida,

[1] Milman.

who also predicts the poet's exile and wanderings, and
in a strain of lofty enthusiasm urges him to pour out all the
heart of his vision and brave the hatred and the persecution
that it will surely bring upon him.

This Cacciaguida was a Crusader who fell in the Holy
Wars, and Dante meets him in the burning planet of Mars,
amongst the mighty warriors of the Lord whose souls
blaze there in a ruddy glow of glory. There is Joshua,
there Judas Maccabæus, and Charlemagne and Orlando
and Godfrey and many more.

A red cross glows athwart the planet's orb, and from
it beams in mystic guise the Christ; but how, the poet
cannot say, for words and images are wanting to portray
it. Yet he who takes his cross and follows Christ, will
one day forgive the tongue that failed to tell what he shall
see when to him also Christ shall flash through that glowing
dawn of light.

Here the souls, like rubies that glow red upon the
gleaming cross as stars shine forth out of the Milky Way,
pass and repass from horn to horn, from base to summit,
and burst into a brighter radiance as they join and cross,
while strains of lofty and victorious praise, unknown to
mortal ears, gather upon the cross as though it were a
harp of many strings, touched by the hand of God, and
take captive the entranced, adoring soul.

There Cacciaguida hailed his descendant Dante, and long
they conversed of the past, the present, and the future. Alas
for our poor pride of birth! What wonder if men glory in it

here? For even there in heaven, where no base appetite distorts the will and judgment, even there did Dante glow with pride to call this man his ancestor.

At last their converse ended; Cacciaguida's soul again was sweeping the unseen strings of that heavenly harp, and Dante turned again to look for guidance from his guardian. Beatrice's eyes were fixed above; and quick as the blush passes from a fair cheek, so quick the ruddy glow of Mars was gone, and the white light of Jupiter shone clear and calm in the sixth Heaven—the Heaven of the Just.

What a storm of passions and emotions swept through Dante's soul when he learnt where he was! "O chivalry of Heaven!" he afterwards exclaims, "pray for those who are led all astray on earth by foul example." When would the Righteous One again be wroth, and purge His temple of the traffickers—His temple walled by miracles and martyrdoms? How long should the Pope be suffered to degrade his holy office by making the penalties of Church discipline the tools of selfish politics—how long should his devotion to St. John the Baptist, whose head was stamped upon the coins of Florence, make him neglect the fisherman and Paul?

Such are the thoughts that rise in Dante's mind when he thinks of the Heaven of the Just; but in that Heaven itself another feeling masters him. Here surely, here if anywhere God's justice must be manifest. Reflected in all heaven, here must it shine without a veil. The spirits of the just could surely solve his torturing doubt. How long had his soul hungered and found no food on earth, and now how eagerly did he wait the answer to his doubt! They knew his doubt, he need not tell it them ; oh, let them solve it !

Yes, they knew what he would say : " A man is born upon the bank of Indus, and there is none to speak of Christ, or read or write of him. All this man's desires and acts are good, and without sin, as far as human eye can see, in deed or word. He dies unbaptised, without the faith. Where is that justice which condemns him ? Where is his fault in not believing ?" Yes, they knew his doubt, but could not solve it. Their answer is essentially the same as Paul's : " Nay, but, O man, who art thou that repliest against God ?"

The Word of God, say the spirits of the just, could not be so expressed in all the universe but what it still remained in infinite excess. Nay, Lucifer, the highest of created beings, could not at once see all the light of God, and fell through his impatience. How then could a poor mortal hope to scan the ways of God? His ken was lost in His deep justice as the eye is lost in the ocean. We can see the shallow bottom at the shore, but we cannot see the bottom of the deep, which none the less is there. So God's unfathomable justice is too deep, too just, for us to comprehend. The Primal Will, all goodness in itself, moves not aside from justice and from good. Never indeed did man ascend to heaven who believed not in Christ, yet there are many who cry, Lord, Lord, and in the day of judgment shall be far more remote from Christ than many a one that knew him not.[1]

[1] *Paradiso*, xiv. 85—xix. 148.

With this answer Dante must be content. He must
return from Heaven with this thirst unslaked, this long
hunger still unsatisfied. Ay, and with this answer must we
too rest content. And yet not with this answer, for we do
not ask this question. That awful load of doubt under which
Dante bent is lifted from our souls, and for us there is
no eternal Hell, no virtuous but rejected Heathen. Yet to
us too the ocean of God's justice is too deep to pierce. And
when we ask why every blessing, every chance of good
is taken from one child, while another is bathed from infancy
in the light of love, and is taught sooner than it can walk to
choose the good, and to reject the evil, what answer can we
have but Dante's? Rest in faith. You know God's justice,
for you feel it with you in your heart when you are fighting
for the cause of justice; you know God's justice, for you feel
it in your heart like an avenging angel when you sin; you
know God's justice, but you do not know it all.

There in the Heaven of the Just was David; now he
knew how precious were his songs, since his reward was such.
There too was Trajan who by experience of the bliss of
Heaven and pain of Hell knew how dear the cost of not
obeying Christ. There were Constantine, and William of
Sicily, and Ripheus, that just man of Troy. "What things
are these?" was the cry that dropped by its own weight from
Dante's lips. The heathens Trajan and Ripheus here! No,
not heathens. Ripheus had so given himself to justice when
on earth, that God in His grace revealed to him the coming

Christ, and he believed. Faith, Hope, and Charity were his baptism more than a thousand years ere baptism was known. And for Trajan, Gregory had wrestled in prayer for him, had taken the kingdom of heaven by storm with his warm love and living hope; and since no man repents in Hell, God at the prayer of Gregory had recalled the imperial soul back for a moment to its mouldering clay. There it believed in Christ, and once more dying entered on his joy.[1]

Thus did Dante wrestle with his faith, and in the passion of his love of virtue and thrist for justice seek to escape the problem which he could not solve.

But we must hasten to the close. Dante and Beatrice have passed through all the heavens. The poet's sight is gradually strengthened and prepared for the supreme vision. He has already seen a kind of symbol of the Uncreated, surrounded by the angelic ministers. It was in the ninth heaven, the Heaven of the Primum Mobile, that he saw a single point of intensest light surrounded by iris rings, upon which points, said Beatrice, all Heaven and all nature hung.[2]

But now they have passed beyond all nine revolving heavens into the region of "pure light, light intellectual full of love, love of the true good full of joy, joy that transcends all sweetness."[3] And here the poet sees that for which all else had been mere preparation.

---

[1] *Paradiso*, xx.   [2] *Ibid.* xxviii, 41, 42.
[3] *Ibid.* xxx. 40-42.

But I will not strive to reproduce his imagery, with the mighty river of light inexhaustible, with the mystic flowers of heavenly perfume, with the sparks like rubies set in gold ever passing between the flowers and the river. Of this light Dante drank, and then the true forms of what had hitherto been shadowed forth in emblems only, rose before his eyes. Rank upon rank the petals of the mystic rose of Paradise stretched far away around and above him. There were the blessed souls of the holy ones, bathed in the light of God that streamed upon them from above, while the angels ever passed between it and them ministering peace and love.

There high up, far, far beyond the reach of mortal eye, had it been on earth, sat Beatrice, who had left the poet's side. But in Heaven, with no destroying medium to intervene, distance is no let to perfect sight. He spoke to her. He poured out his gratitude to her, for it was she who had made him a free man from a slave, she who had made him sane, she who had left her footprints in Hell for him, when she went to summon Virgil to his aid. Oh, that his life hereafter might be worthy of the grace and power that had so worked for him! Then from her distant place in Heaven, Beatrice looked at him and smiled, then turned her eyes upon the Uncreated Light.[1]

St. Bernard was at Dante's side, and prayed that the seer's vision might be strengthened to look on God. Then Dante turned his eyes to the light above. The unutterable glory of that light dazzled not his intent love-guided gaze.

[1] *Paradiso,* xxxi. 59-93.

Nay, rather did it draw it to itself and every moment strengthen it with keener sight and feed it with intenser love.

Deeper and deeper into that Divine Light the seer saw. Had he turned his eyes aside, then indeed he knew the piercing glory would have blinded them ; but that could never be, for he who gazes on that light feels all desire centred there—in it are all things else. So for a time with kindling gaze the poet looked into the light of God, unchanging, yet to the strengthening sight revealing ever more. Mysteries that no human tongue can tell, no human mind conceive, were flashed upon him in the supreme moment, and then all was over—" The power of the lofty vision failed."

Dante does not tell us where he found himself when the vision broke. He only tells us this : that as a wheel moves equally in all its parts, so his desire and will were, without strain or jar, revolved henceforth by that same Love that moves the sun and all the other stars. [1]

This was the end of all that Dante had thought and felt and lived through—a will that rolled in perfect oneness with the will of God. This was the end to which he would bring his readers, this was the purpose of his sacred poem, this was the meaning of his life. [2]

[1] *Paradiso*, xxxiii. 143-145.
[2] Symonds.

APPENDIX

AN ATTEMPT TO STATE THE CENTRAL
THOUGHT OF THE COMEDY

APPENDIX

DANTE's poem—the true reflection of his mind—is a compact and rounded *whole* in which all the parts are mutually interdependent. Its digressions are never excrescences, its episodes are never detached from its main purpose, its form is never arbitrary and accidental, but is always the systematic and deliberate expression of its substance. Moreover it is profoundly mediæval and Catholic in conception and spirit. The scholastic theology and science of the Middle Ages and the spiritual institutions of the Catholic Church were no trammels to Dante's thought and aspiration. Under them and amidst them he moved with a perfect sense of freedom, in them he found the embodiment of his loftiest conceptions. Against their abuses his impetuous spirit poured out its lava-stream of burning indignation, but his very passion against those who laid impure hands upon the sacred things of God is the measure of his reverence for their sanctity.

If the Catholic poet of the fourteenth century speaks with a voice that can reach the ears and stir the hearts of the Protestant and heretic of the nineteenth, it is not so much because he rose above the special forms and conditions of the faith of his own age as because he went below them and touched the eternal rock upon which they rested. Not by neglecting or making light of the dogmas and institutions of his day, but by piercing to their very heart and revealing their deepest foundations, he became a poet for all time.

The distinction, then, which we are about to draw between the permanent realities of Dante's religion and the passing forms, the temporary conditions of belief, under which it was manifested, is a

109

distinction which did not exist for him. His faith was a garment woven without seam, or, to use his own metaphor, a coin so true in weight and metal, so bright and round, that there was no "perhaps" to him in its impression.[1]

This unwavering certainty alike in principle and in detail, this unfaltering loyalty to the beliefs of his days alike in form and substance, is one of the secrets of Dante's strength.

But, again, such compactness and cohesion of belief could not have been attained except by the strict subordination of every article of concrete faith to the great central conceptions of religion, rising out of the very nature and constitution of the devout human soul. And therefore, paradox as it may seem, the very intensity with which Dante embraced beliefs that we have definitely and utterly rejected, is the pledge that we shall find in his teaching the essence of our own religion ; and we may turn to the Comedy with the certainty that we shall not only discover here and there passages which will wake an echo in our bosoms, but shall also find at the very heart of it some guiding thought that will be to us as it was to him, absolutely true.

Now Dante himself, as we have seen, tells us what is the subject of his Comedy. Literally it is "The state of souls after death," and allegorically "Man, as rendering himself liable to rewarding or punishing justice, by good or ill desert in the exercise of his free will." The ideal requirements of Divine Justice, then, form the central subject of this poem, the one theme to which amidst infinite diversity of application, the poet remains ever true ; and these requirements he works out in detail and enforces with all the might, the penetration, the sweetness of his song, under the conditions of mediæval belief as to the future life.

But these conditions of belief are utterly foreign to our own conceptions. I say nothing of the rejection of the virtuous heathen, because Dante himself could really find no room for it in his own system of conceptions. It lay in his mind as a belief accepted from

[1] *Paradiso*, xxiv. 86, 87.

tradition but never really assimilated by faith. Apart from this, however, we find ourselves severed from Dante by his fundamental dogma that the hour of death ends all possibility of repentance or amendment. With him there is no repentance in Hell, no progress in Heaven; and it is therefore only in Purgatory that we find anything at all fundamentally analogous to the modern conception of a progressive approximation to ideal perfection and oneness with God throughout the cycles of a future life. And even here the transition of Purgatory is but temporal, nor is there any fundamental or progressive change of heart in its circles, for unless the heart be changed before death it cannot change at all.

In its literal acceptation, then, dealing with "the state of souls after death," the "Divine Comedy" has little to teach us, except indirectly.

But allegorically it deals with "man," first as impenitently sinful, second, as penitent, last, as purified and holy. It shows us the requirements of Divine Justice with regard to these three states; and whether we regard them as permanent or transitory, as severed by sharp lines one from the other, or as melting imperceptibly into each other, as existing on earth or beyond the grave, in any case Dante teaches us what sentence justice must pronounce on impenitence, on penitence, and on sanctity. Nay, independently of any belief in future retribution at all, independently of any belief in what our actions will receive, Dante burns or flashes into our souls the indelible conviction of what they deserve.

Now to Dante's mind, as to most others, the conceptions of *justice* and *desert* implied the conception of *free will*. And accordingly we find the reality of the choice exercised by man, and attended by such eternal issues, maintained with intense conviction throughout the poem. The free will is the supreme gift of God, and that by which the creature most closely partakes of the nature of the Creator. The free gift of God's love must be seized by an act of man's free will, in opposition to the temptations and difficulties that interpose themselves. There is justice as well as love in Heaven; justice as well as mercy in

Purgatory. The award of God rests upon the free choice of man, and registers his merit or demerit. It is true, and Dante fully recognises it, that one man has a harder task than another. The original constitution and the special circumstances of one man make the struggle far harder for him than for another ; but God never suffers the hostile influence of the stars to be so strong that the human will may not resist it. Diversity of character and constitution is the necessary condition of social life, and we can see why God did not make us all alike ; but when we seek to pierce yet deeper into the mystery of His government, and ask why this man is selected for this task, why another is burdened with that toil, why one finds the path of virtue plain for his feet to tread, while another finds it beset with obstacles before which his heart stands still—when we ask these questions we trench close upon one of those doubts which Dante brought back unsolved from Heaven. Not the seraph whose sight pierces deepest into the light of God could have told him this, so utterly is it veiled from all created sight.[1]

But amidst all these perplexities one supreme fact stands out to Dante's mind ; that, placed as we are on earth amidst the mysterious possibilities of good and evil, we are endowed with a genuine power of self-directed choice between them. The fulness of God's grace is freely offered to us all, the life eternal of obedience, of self-surrender, of love, tending ever to the fuller and yet fuller harmony of united will and purpose, of mutually blessed and blessing offices of affection, of growing joy in all the supporting and surrounding creation, of growing repose in the might and love of God.

But if we shut our eyes against the light of God's countenance and turn our backs upon His love, if we rebel against the limitations of mutual self-sacrifice to one another and common obedience to God, then an alternative is also offered us in the fierce and weltering chaos of wild passions and disordered desires, recognising no law and evok-

[1] Compare *Purgatorio*, xvi. 67-84 ; *Paradiso*, iv. 73-114, v. 13 sqq., viii. 115-129, xxi. 76-102, xxxii. 49-75.

ing no harmony, striking at the root of all common purpose and cut off from all helpful love.

Our inmost hearts recognise the reality of this choice, and the justice and necessity of the award that gives us what we have chosen. That the hard, bitter, self-seeking, impure, mutinous, and treacherous heart should drive away love and peace and joy, is the natural, the necessary result of the inmost nature and constitution of things, and our hearts accept it. That self-discipline, gentleness, self-surrender, devotion, generosity, self-denying love, should gather round them light and sweetness, should infuse a fulness of joy into every personal and domestic relation, should give a glory to every material surrounding, and should gain an ever closer access to God, is no artificial arrangement which might with propriety be reversed, it is a part of the eternal and necessary constitution of the universe, and we feel that it ought so to be.

There is no joy or blessedness without harmony, there is no harmony without the concurrence of independent forces, there is no such concurrence without self-discipline and self-surrender.

But these natural consequences of our moral action are here on earth constantly interfered with and qualified, constantly baulked of their full and legitimate effect. Here we do not get our deserts. The actions of others affect us almost as much as our own, and artificially interpose themselves to screen us from the results of what we are and do ourselves. Hence we constantly fail to perceive the true nature of our choice. Its consequences fall on others; we partially at least evade the Divine Justice, and forget or know not what we are doing, and what are the demands of justice with regard to us.

Now Dante, in his three poems, with an incisive keenness of vision and a relentless firmness of touch, that stand alone, strips our life and our principles of action of all these distracting and confusing surroundings, isolates them from all qualifying and artificial palliatives, and shows us what our choice is, and where it leads to.

In Hell we see the natural and righteous results of sin, recognise the direct consequences, the fitting surroundings of a sinful life, and understand what the sinful choice in its inmost nature is. As surely as our consciences accuse us of the sins that are here punished, so surely do we feel with a start of self-accusing horror, "This is what I am trying to make the world. This is where I should be lodged if I received what I have given. This is what justice demands that I should have. This is what I deserve. It is what I *have chosen*."

The tortures of Hell are not artificial inflictions, they are simply the reflection and application of the sinner's own ways and principles. He has made his choice, and he is given that which he has chosen. He has found at last a world in which his principles of action are not checked and qualified at every turn by those of others, in which he is not screened from any of the consequences of his deeds, in which his own life and action has consolidated, so to speak, about him, and has made his surroundings correspond with his heart.

In the Hell, Dante shows us the nature and the deserts of impenitent sin ; and though we may well shrink from the ghastly conception of an eternal state of impenitence and hatred, yet surely there is nothing from which we ought to shrink in the conception of impenitent sin as long as it lasts, whether in us or in others, concentrating its results upon itself, making its own place, and therefore receiving its deserts.

When we turn from Hell to Purgatory, we turn from unrepentant and therefore constantly cherished, renewed, and reiterated sin, to repentant sin, already banished from the heart. What does justice demand with regard to such sin? Will it have it washed out? Will it, in virtue of the sinner's penitence, intervene between him and the wretched results and consequences of his deeds? Who that has ever sinned and repented will accept for a moment such a thought? The repentant sinner does not *wish* to escape the consequences and results of his sin. His evil deeds or passions must bring and ought to bring a long trail of wretched suffering for himself. This suffering is not corrective, it is expiatory. His heart is already corrected, it is already turned in shame and penitence to God; but if he had no punishment, if his evil deed brought no suffering upon himself, he would feel that the Divine Justice had been outraged. He shrinks from the thought with a hurt sense of moral unfitness. He wishes to suffer; he would not escape into the peace of Heaven if he might.

Never did Dante pierce more deeply into the truth of things, never did he bring home the *justice* of punishment more closely to the heart, than when he told how the souls in Purgatory do not wish to rise to Heaven till they have worked out the consequences of their sins. The sin long since repented and renounced still haunts us with its shame and its remorse, still holds us from the fulness of the joy of God's love, still smites us with a keener pain the closer we press into the forgiving Father's presence; and we would have it so. The deepest longing of our heart, which is now set right, is for full untroubled communion with God, yet it is just when nearest to Him that we feel the wretched penalty of our sin most keenly and that we least desire to escape it.

But if the sinful disposition be gone, then the source of our suffering is dried up with it, and the sense of oneness with God, of harmony and trust, gradually overpowers the self-reproach, until from the state of penitence and suffering the soul rises to holiness and peace.

It is in giving us glimpses of this final state that Dante wields his most transforming power over our lives. He shows us what God offers us, what it is that we have hitherto refused, what it is that we may still aspire to, that here or hereafter we may hope to reach. Sin-stained and sorrow-laden as we are, it is only on wings as strong as his that we can be raised even for a moment into that Divine blessedness in which sin has been so purged by suffering, so dried up by the sinner's love of God, so blotted out by God's love of him, that it has vanished as a dream, and the soul can say, "Here we repent not."[1]

[1] *Paradiso*, ix. 103.

How mighty the spirit that can raise us even for a moment from the desolate weariness of Hell, and the long suffering of Purgatory, to the joy and peace of Heaven!

And here too there is justice. Here too the deserts of the soul are the gauge of its condition. For, as we have seen, in the very blessedness of Heaven, there are grades, and the soul which has once been stained with sin or tainted with selfish and worldly passion, can never be as though it had been always pure. Yet the torturing sense of unworthiness is gone, the unrest of a past that thwarts the present is no more; the souls have cast off the burden of their sin, and are at perfect peace with God and with themselves.

Sin, repentance, holiness, confronted with the Eternal Justice— what they are and what they deserve—such is the subject of Dante Alighieri's Comedy.

Have nigh six centuries of progress out-grown the poem, or are Dante's still the mightiest and most living words in which man has ever painted in detail the true deserts of sin, of penitence, of sanctity? The growing mind of man has burst the shell of Dante's mediæval creed. Is his portrayal of the true conditions of blessedness as antiquated as his philosophy, his religion as strange to modern thought as his theology? Or has he still a power, wielded by no other poet, of taking us into the very presence of God and tuning our hearts to the harmonies of Heaven? Those who have been with him on his mystic journey, and have heard and seen, can answer the questions with a declaration as clear and ringing as the poet's own confession of faith in the courts of Heaven. If those who have but caught some feeble echoes of his song can partly guess what the true answer is, then those echoes have not been waked in vain.

INDEX

OF REFERENCES TO DANTE'S WORKS IN

FOOT-NOTES

INDEX

1